MASTERING NETWORK

MARKETING:
APPROACHES

PROVEN

FROM GREATS

FROM BASICS TO BRILLIANCE:
PROVEN STRATEGIES FOR SUCCESS

MASTERING NETWORK MARKETING: PROVEN APPROACHES FROM GREATS

FROM BASICS TO BRILLIANCE: PROVEN STRATEGIES FOR SUCCESS

BY: ROB SPERRY

TGON Publishing

TGON Publishing

CONTENTS

INTRODUCTION

Welcome to "Mastering Network Marketing: Proven Approaches from Greats." In an ever-evolving industry, achieving success requires more than just determination; it demands proven strategies, insights from seasoned professionals, and a willingness to adapt and grow. This book is designed to be your comprehensive guide, providing you with the tools and knowledge you need to excel in the competitive world of network marketing.

Throughout my career, I've had the privilege of learning from some of the best minds in the industry. Their experiences, wisdom, and innovative approaches have been instrumental in shaping my journey, and it is this collective expertise that I aim to share with you. Whether you're just starting out or looking to take your business to the next level, the strategies and stories in this book will offer valuable lessons and actionable steps to help you reach your goals.

Remember, success in network marketing isn't just about the destination; it's about the journey. Embrace each challenge as an opportunity to grow, and let the insights from these industry greats inspire you to create your own path to success.

"No one is you, and that is your
SUPERPOWER!"

– Unknown

ALICIA WILLIAMS

- Native of Alabama, currently residing in Georgia with her husband and three children: one daughter and two sons.

- In network marketing for ten years.

- Former Educator who retired herself before the age of 40 from a 15-year career in the field after only two years in the business.

- Top .01 percent in her company, six-figure earner award for FIVE consecutive years.

- Leads a team of over 100,000 consultants.

- Signature necklace, "The Alicia," named in her honor.

- First African American Elite Leader in her company. She shares hope and empowers her team to walk in their own greatness.

5 Effective Ways To Stay Motivated and Win On Purpose

I am pretty sure that William Shakespeare was talking about me when he boldly wrote, "And though she be little, she is fierce!" If you can believe in yourself, you will become unstoppable at whatever you decide to accomplish. Everything that I have set out to achieve on this journey started with the choice to BELIEVE in myself.

One of my careers was as a college program director on a very well-known college campus. As the youngest person who had ever done this job, I was immediately looked at by my now fellow peers, who were much older, as unworthy or undeserving of such a position. There was no one to turn to that saw me as deserving or believed in me. I was forced to find my voice and believe that I did deserve it. I knew I was qualified and that I was the right person for the role. I had to have my own back and know that I believed in ME, and no one else mattered. In this chapter, you will learn how to stay motivated and win on purpose, even when others doubt who you are and what you can achieve.

#1 What's Your Superpower?

> *"No one is you,*
> *and that is your Superpower."*
>
> *— Unknown*

Knowing who you are and whose you are matters. We are all wonderfully and fearfully made. We are all capable of our own unique contributions to this world. Who are you? What sets you apart from everyone else? You must identify the intangible skills that set you apart from the rest of this world. These skills could be, for example, a strong work ethic, being a person of high integrity, or being someone who keeps their word. It is important that you know for yourself who you are and what sets you apart.

There will always be someone better or smarter than you, but NO one is YOU! Surround yourself with others who see greatness in you and who will push you to level up. But, as I mentioned before, the most important thing is that you see greatness in yourself first. Greatness looks different for all of us. Some of us may have amazing listening skills or the ability to believe in others. Someone else may have the gift of sales and motivating people. Don't focus on what skills you don't have. Don't focus your attention on trying to be the next Michael Jordan or Kobe Bryant in your industry, but instead be the next YOU. Be yourself and know that YOU are your own superpower.

As a former educator, teaching is a work of heart. Many have been blessed with the gift to inspire and empower others to greatness. It is an educator's superpower. When my students wanted to give up or throw in the towel, I stepped in with words of encouragement letting them know that nothing was impossible for those who believe. I remember seeing one student in particular, who was struggling. I knew that he had the capability to be more and do more, but he was showing up lacking the confidence and motivation to see his potential. I saw him wanting to give up on himself, and that just wouldn't cut it for him. I sat him down and gave him a glimpse of what I saw in him. I gave him the bigger picture, not just a test score on a sheet of paper. That changed everything for him. The way his confidence shot through the roof after that conversation was life-changing for him and for me. Up to this point, I hadn't seen that I had a superpower. I had just thought that I cared and was passionate about what I was doing. But when I watched this particular student grow and change, that was when I knew what my superpower was. I was incredible at inspiring and empowering others to believe in themselves.

As an entrepreneur, knowing and identifying your strengths (superpower) will push or carry you through when tough times arise. We often see the good in others and can identify their strengths, but we can struggle to see our own. It is so important that you take the time to see what your superpowers are. Although some will encourage you, it will ultimately be up to you to always know your strengths and work on nurturing them. In this industry, your success is totally up to you. The harsh reality is no one is coming to save you. You must do the saving all on your own. You must posture up, believe that it's possible, put on your cape, and go get it!

Coach Rob's Notes: "Alicia nailed it. "Knowing and identifying your strengths (superpower) will push or carry you through when tough times arise." This sentence summed up so much. First off, notice how Alicia said WHEN rather than IF. Tough times will arise. Next, she understands that we have our most success from our strengths. Double down on those strengths and make them even better because they are what make you unique."

#2 Mindset Matters - Adopting a Champion Mindset

"The mind is everything.
What you think you become."

– Buddha

Can you see it? Can you see yourself succeeding and creating the life of your dreams? Can you see yourself walking the stage to receive the award you got from your company? Can you see yourself helping to change the lives of others around you? Before you accomplish anything, you must first see yourself as a success. In the network marketing industry, many have doubted if they could have the success they desire. They will start to doubt if they made the right choice by choosing to sign up with a company. Or, maybe you wonder if the product you are selling is really what you want to be selling and if this is the right choice for you. Have you ever said to yourself, "Oh boy, what did I get myself into?"

You may even let other people and their opinions and judgments get into your head. The Negative Nancy and the Bad Attitude Bob tell you that it is not possible, and you start to believe them! This happens! But you have to come back to yourself and remember that you said yes to this opportunity and network marketing for a reason. You ultimately believe in the brand, the vision, and the products. It doesn't matter what other people think or say. Your passion will be contagious to others when you remind yourself and start to act from your superpowers. This burning passion or desire will push you to no limits in believing you can achieve your dreams and goals.

Over the years, I've pushed for next-level rank advancements and company incentive trips. I have achieved many but have also fallen short with some. One of the biggest lessons I have learned from all of my experiences was to never throw in the towel too fast. Fight until the end. Some of my biggest accomplishments happened in the eleventh hour. If I would have given up when I thought it wasn't going to work out, I would have been guaranteeing that I would not reach the goal. But not throwing in the towel too fast enabled me to work hard and go all-in on myself. This is a champion's mindset. The race is not given to the swift or strong, but to the one who endures to the end. In the network marketing business, you will experience failure after failure after failure. In these times, you are not losing; you are learning.

Success in network marketing is a journey. On this journey, you must have heart. Prepare for the heartbreaks, disappointments, lack of support, and setbacks. When others give up on you, just make sure you don't give up on yourself. If at first, you don't succeed, pick yourself up and try again. Get back on the front line and give it all you've got. No one said it would be easy; it's worth it. You are worth it. Your family is worth it! The victory in network marketing is having the mindset of a champion. Believing in yourself even when no one else does.

#3 The Power of Your Story

"In order to win a man to your cause,
you must first reach his heart,
the great high road to his reason."

— Abraham Lincoln

As you have often heard before, people don't buy products; they buy people. You can no longer tell people how you made it happen, you must show them. Who are you? What do you have to offer them? In the words of Tom Cruise, "show me the money"! They simply want to know how they can get to the money and get it fast. We know there's no elevator to success, you must take the stairs.

People connect with people who inspire or motivate them through similar life experiences. What were your struggles and hardships? What sacrifices did you make along the way? How did you push past the pain? Facts tell, but stories sell and connect to the masses. If you want others to connect, you must connect with them by being your authentic self. Don't be ashamed of your story; it will inspire others. Have you ever read someone's story and thought, "This is exactly what I needed to hear today?" Your story will do that for someone else.

I often think of my early years in my current company. At times, I was ashamed or somewhat embarrassed to share what I was currently doing on the side in network marketing and that I had to supplement my income to feed my shopping habit. I dare not wear this as a professional, let alone sell it. Although my salary was not bad at all, within the first two years of being with this company, I was able to retire from my career of 15 years. My message to you is to never be ashamed of your side hustle; no one is going to feed you if you go broke.

Don't allow others to downplay what you're doing. Share your story; it's bigger than you. Someone is counting on you. Be a beacon of light and inspiration to others, a hope dealer. We know many are skeptics of our industries; however, being transparent by sharing your story, your humble beginnings, and showing up as your authentic self will connect you with the right individuals.

Coach Rob's Notes: "One of the biggest clichés in network marketing is that facts tell and stories sell. It is 100% true and will always be true. We love a good movie or book because of the story it tells. All too often, network marketers skip this vital step of improving their communication/storytelling. I can tell you based on experience that storytelling was a major weakness of mine. It took me years of focus and paying attention to other great storytellers to learn how to tell a better story. I felt uncomfortable showing emotion. I left out the important details. I also felt that I didn't have a powerful story. That is never true. Each one of you has a very powerful story. You just need to learn how to tell it, which will come from deliberate practice."

#4 You Are Your Own Competition

"Comparison is the thief of joy."

— Theodore Roosevelt

Look in the mirror... that's your competition. It's you vs. you. Your only focus is being better than the person you were yesterday. Your journey to achieving your goals or having the success that you desire is your race at your pace. You can't compare your chapter three to someone else's chapter thirty three. Your vision and goals may align with others, but your journey will be different.

My ten years in network marketing have taught me to stay in my lane with a focus on helping others achieve their goals. This industry is designed so that we all can win. You can outrank your upline, or your team members can outrank you. I have been on both sides of surpassing my upline in rank, but have also had team members within my downline outrank me too. It is one of the best parts of network marketing. Your journey to success is your own and not paced by someone else.

On your journey to success in this industry, your competition is procrastination, your ego, the knowledge you neglect, a negative mindset, and your lack of creativity. Compete against that. It's never about being the best; it's about being better than who you were yesterday. Bet on you!

#5 The SWSWSWSW Philosophy

"Don't worry about being successful but work towards being significant, and the success will naturally follow."

— Oprah Winfrey

Entrepreneurship is not for the faint of heart. Network Marketing is not for everyone, but everyone can do it. Building a business can be tough, and you will inevitably encounter rejection and disappointment from prospects, team members, and family and friends. Don't trip and don't quit. Take a breather and remember: Some Will Some Won't So What Show up and Work.

Coach Rob's Notes: "I absolutely love this phrase that Alicia shared. "Some Will Some Won't So What Show up and Work."This phrase gives us more perspective on the process of success, which ultimately leads to success. All too often, we focus solely on results. Yes, results can be an indicator, but they aren't the only indicator. For example, if you sign up five people next week and they all quit, are you bad at network marketing? Let's go further. Let's say after they quit, you don't get any better, but the following week you sign up just one person. That one person then goes and signs up ten people in the business. Are you better or worse than you were the week before? You are exactly the same, but based on the results, you think you are better or worse. Managing your emotions is one of the biggest keys to success in network marketing.

Stop trying to convince people that this is the opportunity for them. Don't tell; show them. Take them on your journey often to show how this business is positively impacting your life and your team members. Show the fun and exciting things happening. Ignore the noise of the naysayers and dream busters. Focus your time and energy on those who are happy for you, and inspire and motivate you to continue to grow.

Dear Entrepreneur,

You've entered the fastest-growing business model, Network Marketing. This is your season to walk in your greatness! Be confident and believe in who you are, fight for what you desire, inspire others through your journey, compete with no one but yourself, and stay positive through it all.

Let's Go, Grow and Glow!

"Be the change you wish

to see in the world."

– Unknown

AMBER BRILL

- Full-time network marketer with multiple 7-figure online business.

- Earned 25 free trips through a 18-year career.

- Personally recruited over 1,200 business partners

- Coached and developed multiple 6 figure earners.

- Featured in several publications.

- Current network marketing business has over 35,000 customers and 1,900 team members.

Shifting and Changing

I started over eighteen years ago in a party planning company in the network marketing industry. My main goal when I started was to do something fun to get out of the house. I was a new stay-at-home mom with a precious baby girl. While I loved being at home with her, I missed the interaction with people all day that I had in my corporate job. Now, don't get me wrong, I loved being home and not missing a single moment in my baby girl's life; I just missed the adults that could talk with me. Money wasn't why I got started; I just wanted fun and people. I found a company doing at-home purse parties on Craigslist and decided to join up. At the time, I would have never imagined that this fun thing I was doing to get out of the house would turn into a full-time income.

Life has an interesting way of shifting and changing. Five years ago, I found myself in a challenging position. My previous network marketing company wasn't going well. I found myself a single mom in my personal life after recently divorcing. I couldn't pay my bills, even though I worked sixty hours a week. I was embarrassed to talk about what I thought was a complete disaster in life and business. My closest friends and family didn't even know what I was going through. It felt too big and embarrassing to admit, but now I realize how many people go through something similar to what I did. I realized that when I shared my struggles with others, I was in a position to help others move forward in their own lives. But to do that, I had to overcome my fears of being embarrassed and feeling judged. I am so glad that I did. I started making empowering decisions for my own life and creating the change that I needed to succeed. The very best part for me is that I can inspire others to keep going and make their wildest dreams come true as well.

Your reasons for doing this business will change over time. It can change from wanting to have fun and talking to people to needing a full-time income that can support you and your family. I fell in love with the industry for what it did for me being a stay-at-home mom. I quickly realized that network marketing could become a lot more than just a hobby. Network marketing was an opportunity to change my life, my future, and build a business and the income that would help me empower and help other people do the same.

Your story will not always be the same. As you reach milestones in your career, your story will change, and you will end up with multiple layers of your story to share to increase the impact on your audience based on where they are in their life.

Coach Rob's Notes: "Does your why make you cry? When I first started, my why hadn't been found. I felt a little guilty thinking about what is wrong with me. As my time in the business grew, so did my why and purpose. Eventually, it became clear, but I always had to be open to things shifting and changing. Change is inevitable. The most important thing is how you deal with it."

Stand Out From The Crowd

There are so many people online with businesses; it's really important to stand out and be yourself. The ultimate goal is to stand out online and make a huge positive impact with a ripple effect for millions. You want to share the good, the bad, and the ugly guys. You may read this and think, "Oh yeah, but Amber doesn't mean it." Let me say it again. Share the good, the bad, AND the ugly. Sharing is what makes excellent connections with others. No one lives in the "Instagram Life," where everything is vacations, parties, and epic experiences. Sharing my story has helped me create a legacy for my family. I've turned my mess into my message and have helped so many others create a path towards improving their lives by doing the same. Never be afraid to share the struggles and less-than-perfect moments of your life. But more importantly, what you did to navigate your way through those struggles, to find yourself in a better place on the other side.

Social media can be such a powerful tool and impactful in people's lives when used in the right way. The problem with social media these days is that so many focus on the highlights of their lives and paint a picture, showing their best moments. And that's often viewed as unrealistic to their audience. We can use social media every day through life's highs and the lows. So why not showcase everything in your life to make an impact and allow your story to help others succeed and overcome their struggles as well. Showing the glamorous life and not telling them how you got there and the struggles you had to overcome doesn't provide any benefit or value to your audience. Studies show that social media can often influence people in a negative way, leading others to feel down about themselves, and as if everyone has a better life than you do. It's always been a really important goal for me to keep my social media realistic, honest, fun, helpful, and never try to paint a picture-perfect life because, really does one even exist?

I often show up messy with my baby in tow, the puppy biting us, and a teenager that is, well, a teenager. But I humbly share my story of where I was, what changes I made, and how I showed up consistently to build the empire I'm so blessed to have. And finally, how I got to the point of my life and created the success that I always desired, to have the money to do what I want when I want, and the time freedom to do the things with my family and make those memories.

I pour into others daily to uplift them, breathe life, and let them know that their past does not define them. I share the message that their present does not determine their future and that anything is possible with hard work, determination, a good attitude, and consistency. Creating a powerful story that's relatable to many is the key to standing out on social media. Your story has the power to impact millions of lives if you are sharing all of it. This can be done with a simple strategy beginning with where you came from and what was your struggle. After that, let your audience know how you overcame that struggle. And finally, what was your end result? Everyone has a story, and we should be able to share that story with the world to relate, inspire and empower.

Coach Rob's Notes: "Standing out from the crowd was hard for me the first few years in network marketing. I was so scared that I didn't even make one post on social media pertaining to anything alluding to network marketing, and this was even after I had hit the top ranks in the company. But here is what I learned and why Amber's last paragraph is so important. Attention is the #1 currency in marketing. Here is the key—attention with the right intention. I think of the people I look up to. Jesus Christ, Gandhi, Mother Teresa, and Martin Luther King Jr., Each one of them had to have some sort of attention in order to create the lasting impact they did. They all did it with the right intention."

Simple, Short, and To The Point

Our story should be told really in less than three minutes, short, simple, and to the point. The more powerful your story is, and the more often you tell it, the more lives you will impact. I suggest staying true to yourself, both in-person and online. Authenticity helps create an audience that knows, likes, and trusts you. If you are the same person online as you are in real life, people will respect that and want to get to know you. You never want to pretend to be someone that you are not or try to be someone else. Be you and attract the tribe that you desire.

When you first start this industry, it can sometimes be hard to let yourself be vulnerable and authentic. You may even be embarrassed by the current situation you're in or your past. I often hear many are worried about sharing their success story, afraid they will come off as bragging. I promise you this is not the case. I feel like that is a really big objection for new people to start sharing their stories, but I want you to know that whatever your struggles are and what you will overcome will help somebody else. When you share your true authentic self, it will speak to many, from your struggle to success. Staying humble is key and never forget where you came from.

I see many people in businesses that are constantly spamming their pages with products, with "buy this," or "buy that," which is not an effective strategy. People will do business with those they know, like, and trust and who are relatable to them. So by sharing your story, maybe not only your business story of where you were before, how you got to where you are now and what you've achieved, sharing a story of products is also important. If you can show someone the benefits of what the product you are currently selling or marketing and how it will help their life, I feel like that is important.

I feel that it's important to share your story authentically and be yourself, both in-person and online. So, as you're sharing and being your authentic self, there's really no difference between sharing your story online or being in person. If you're sharing your story the same as you would when talking to your best friend in person, it will come across the same way whenever you're sharing it online. You can share your story by doing that in your social media posts, in your stories, reels, you can share where you were, where you are now, how you overcame that to get to where you are. As you're sharing and being your authentic self, there's no difference in sharing your story online or being in person.

Sharing my story has taken my business from being just a small business to make a little extra money, to help support bills, to building an online multimillion-dollar empire, where it has not only impacted my life but has impacted the lives of thousands of others by teaching them to share their story and be their authentic self as well.

Network marketing has changed my life. I came here for a little extra money and found myself in a horrible position over five years ago. Now I have a multimillion-dollar business. I am home with my children full time, but I've also been able to retire my fiancé. So both of us are home 24/7.

If you are just starting in this industry, I strongly advise sitting down and taking some time to figure out your goals, where you want to be, and where you see yourself in three, five or ten years? How is this industry going to help you and impact the lives of others? What is the current struggle that you want to overcome? Maybe it's money, maybe it's confidence, or just to make an impact. Figure out what you were before, where you're starting now, and what you're going to do to get to where you want to be so your story can impact as many others as possible.

A great story contains conflict and pain. Start by sharing your background, then share the solution to the conflict or pain you struggled with. Then share how you feel about your future and how much of your life has changed.

Once you have your story nailed down, practice telling it, and do that often! The more you tell your story, the better you will become. The more excitement you will have in your voice and the bigger the impact you will make. You never know how your stories impact others until you share them daily.

If I can go from being a broke single mom to a successful online entrepreneur by sharing my story in a true and authentic way on social media, I know that you can too!

Coach Rob's Notes: "There was one part that hit home for me. Amber said, "I feel that it's important to share your story authentically and be yourself, both in-person and online. So, as you're sharing and being your authentic self, there's really no difference between sharing your story online or being in person." You may think this is common sense, but it isn't. When one tries to be someone else online, and it doesn't match them, things never end well. Your goal on social media is to do a good enough job of showing who you are to the point that if someone met you in person for the first time, they would feel like they already know you."

"Wealth is the ability to fully experience life."

— Henry David Thoreau

ANDREW LOGAN

- 12 years in the NWM Industry.

- Leads a team of 70,000 in 13 countries.

- Multiple 7 Figure Earner.

- Top 3 Company Income Earner.

- Author of *The Way Out* and *The Way Out Together*.

The Residual Myth

'Residual Income' – two of the sexiest words in the Network Marketing industry. Pair them with 'Financial Freedom' and we start to really stir hopes and dreams of a different life. This incredible opportunity to build a business from home, earn residual income and create financial freedom – it's a golden goose that can change our lives forever.

But there's also a rather large elephant in the room here; a lot of people fail to reach their freedom goals. They have an extraordinary vehicle at their fingertips but never manage to make it to their destination. Despite their vision and excitement, they don't get to where they want to be and end up quitting.

It's because they're missing an essential piece of the puzzle – a roadmap. They have a vision, excitement and potential – and are earning extra money. But the final directions to setting yourself free are missing; and that's what I want to help you with.

Coach Rob's Notes: "Having a roadmap is essential. In my own journey, I've seen many people with immense potential fall short because they didn't have a clear direction. It's not just about having the vision, but also about knowing the exact steps to take. Make sure you have a detailed plan and constantly revisit it to stay on track."

Think about your journey to financial freedom like a road trip. With any road trip there are essentials that you need. First and foremost, a vehicle – your company, its products and compensation plan.

Secondly, a destination. You need to know where you want to go. However you define freedom, whatever it looks like for you – you need to know exactly where you want to be in order to set a course for driving there. You also need fuel in the tank; the vision and 'why' that fuels you through each day. As a bonus, you need some companions; a team of people to help take care of the driving at times when you need to rest.

The final ingredient, and the most important in achieving freedom, is the road map. Providing people with systems and scripts helps them launch. They can quickly learn how to drive the car and start their road-trip almost immediately. Having tools and processes in place creates more leverage, supercharging the car with a more powerful engine so you can really put your foot on the gas. Having a team means more people to help you drive – as well as having more fun along the way too.

All of these things allow you to drive faster and further; but it's still very easy to be going the wrong way fast. The faster you drive, the more important it is to know the roads really well. Otherwise, the risk of taking the wrong exit, hitting a detour or (touch wood) having an accident start to rapidly increase.

Personally, there's no better roadmap to wealth creation than Robert Kiyosaki's *Cashflow Quadrant*. He's primarily known for *Rich Dad, Poor Dad*, but it wasn't until I read *Cashflow Quadrant* that everything came together for me.

I had spent most of my 20's battling away, consistently trying (and failing) to create freedom. I had read Kiyosaki's books and had that vision in my mind – I just hadn't found the right vehicle to take me there yet.

Then, in 2012, I was introduced to Network Marketing. And once the penny dropped on how to use Network Marketing to go through the Quadrant – everything changed for my wife and me. We had the roadmap and the vehicle – and our lives forever changed.

So, let me show you how we did it...

Stage 1: Active Income

Kiyosaki calls his first quadrant the 'E' quadrant for Employee. People who are stuck on the proverbial 'hamster wheel' selling time for money; destined to repeat the same day over and over for forty to fifty years; hopefully retiring at the end with whatever they've saved.

He labels it an 'Employee' Quadrant, but really, it's about an active income. Being paid directly for what the time you give or the service you provided. Essentially, if you do X, you will be paid $Y.

When we first launch, it's no different. In the 'side-hustle' stage, we are paid an active income. We see the future of leverage and residual – but if you don't open your mouth, you don't get paid. If there's no prospecting and enrolling – there's no commissions.

To really nail this stage, you need to focus on 4 key actions:

- **Networking**: Learning how to connect with people.

- **Marketing**: Providing value and sharing what you do.

- **Sales**: Taking them from interested to enrolled.

- **Customer Service**: Ensuring they're getting great results and want to continue.

Scripts, systems, tools and templates can do a lot of the heavy lifting here, and one of the very best things about Network Marketing is that we can build our business however we want. Whether it's online or offline, prospecting or attracting, products or opportunity, whichever way you like – focus on building these four skills, and doing them daily, so you can start earning your first cheques. Then, turn around and help others do the same. Or, as we like to call it, Duplication.

Coach Rob's Notes: "Duplication is the backbone of network marketing success. It's crucial to not only master these four skills yourself but also to effectively teach them to your team. Consistent daily actions and a strong duplication system will ensure sustained growth and stability in your business."

Stage 2: Leveraged Income

Labeled the 'S' quadrant for Self-Employed / Small Business Owner by Kiyosaki, this is when we step into our entrepreneurial spirit and start working for ourselves. Looking through a financial lens, this is where we create Leverage – and that is the powerful engine that drives our vehicle forward.

In the traditional working world, leverage is essentially created through having staff. When I had my Physiotherapy clinic, I could only treat so many patients per day. There were only so many hours, and I only had so many hands. By bringing in staff, I could start to create leverage. More patients were able to be seen, more revenue could come into the practice. But there were also limits to this leverage. I could only fit so many staff in the building, there were only so many people in our local area, and I could only afford so many staff members before profits were eaten up.

In Network Marketing, those shackles are removed. Thanks to social media, there's no limit to the number of people we can connect with. Thanks to Zoom, there's no limit to the number of people we can train. Thanks to a global marketplace, there's no limit to the size of the team we can build. The only limits – our business and time management skills. We don't rise to the level of our skills, we fall to the level of our incompetence. The size of the team we can build will ultimately be limited by one thing: our systems.

Systems are essential in creating leverage in a business. More leverage equals more results, which equals more money. It also requires better skills to handle – otherwise we crash; a faster car requires better steering. Unfortunately, this is where a lot of people hit their limit. They can launch a team on pure hustle and energy, but the lack of systems and structure means it eventually collapses. Or they eventually collapse from exhaustion. Creating Systems is the primary skill required to work your way through Stage 2 and onto Stage 3.

At a bare minimum, you need to create systems for the following:

- **Customer Retention**: showing them how to get results so they re-order.

- **Customer Acquisition**: helping new people find their first customers.

- **Distributor Launch**: how to launch your business and earn your first cheque.

- **Distributor Retention**: teaching them how to transition from warm market launch to cold market growth.

- **Recognition**: letting people know you're seeing their hard work.

- **Team Communication**: people are like phones – they need to be regularly plugged in to work at their best.

If you don't have any of these (yet), it may seem a bit overwhelming. But if you spent a month creating each system, you'd completely revolutionize your business within half a year. You'd build an incredible foundation for your business, ready to move towards Stage 3.

There other skill required to really nail Stage 2 is Promotion.

Customers can only take advantage of sales if they know about them. Distributors can only enrol if they know what script to follow. People can only attend events if they know that they're happening.

Events themselves are a system, and an incredible tool of leverage for your business. They allow your team to be trained by the best and inspired from the top – as long as they're there in the room. The skill of promoting the event; getting bums in the room or on the Zoom is one of the highest paying skills in Network Marketing. It is imperative in building a large team, without the stress and overwhelm of 1:1 coaching or mentoring.

Leverage allows you to accelerate the money you're earning, without having to sacrifice more time – taking you one step closer to freedom. But we're not there yet... and stepping from Stage 2 to Stage 3 presents the biggest challenge in creating freedom.

Stage 3: Residual Income

In *The Cashflow Quadrant*, Kiyosaki talks about getting yourself from the left-hand side over to the right-hand side. Away from a job or self-employment and over into business and investment practices. But few people manage to cross that bridge due to a lack of two very important things: time and money.

Network Marketing provides the solution to these problems – but few people manage to solve it. The step from Stage 2 to 3 is the hardest step for most, it's the part of the journey where most people get stuck or lost. The keys to getting there: a mindset shift and a couple of very powerful, and valuable, systems.

We love to use the B word of 'Business' when we're in Stage 2. But the reality is that you don't have a business in Stage 2, it's 'solopreneurship'. You're laying the foundations of a business, but ultimately, it still all rises and falls with you. Systems are incredibly powerful – but like anything, they also have a major weakness. Because when people are following your scripts, following your templates, following your systems – they're doing exactly that, following. They're dependent on you – and there's no leadership created from followship. They'll do plenty of work – so long as you show them what to do.

Leaders, by definition, love to lead. They love to do things their own way and blaze their own trail. Which also means they won't follow your systems – because they're leaders, not followers. It's what makes them so great and also what makes them so challenging.

Without leaders, there's no true residual income or freedom. As good as your systems are, they still require you to evolve them as your company and the market evolves. They still require you to promote and train them – otherwise they stop working. In Stage 2, we can get lulled into a false sense of security thinking our leverage is actually residual - and then take our foot off the gas too soon.

Leverage allows us to earn great amounts of money from small amounts of effort – we can control the rocket ship with the tips of our fingers. Having 1,000 people on a Zoom call is incredible leverage. You're getting 1,000x leverage of your time thanks to that tool. But the team is still dependent on you to run the call. If you stop showing up, so do they. You can make a lot of money through leading followers, but you can never totally switch off. A team of dependent followers can help you leave the workplace, you can travel the world and have a lot more time and choice. But you can't truly step away and enjoy 'freedom' until they're independent of you.

In order to cross this bridge, you need to move from a team of dependent followers to building independent leaders. This mindset shift is the biggest roadblock for so many – because it involves slowing down for a moment and re-tooling. It involves getting out of the way and letting others overtake you. Without it, you will eventually burn-out. You can only push that engine so hard before it produces smoke and breaks down.

Understanding the need to move from leading followers to leading leaders is what will take you through Stage 3, and you do that by having 2 very important systems:

- A Leadership Identification System

- A Leadership Training System

As discussed above, systems and leaders generally clash; it's like pushing the proverbial square peg through a round hole. Paradoxically, the people who often frustrate us with their refusal to follow the system are the exact future leaders we're looking for. The people who follow everything we lay out are amazing, they become pillars of the community and the glue that holds the team together – but rarely do they become leaders.

This is why a system for identifying the leaders becomes essential in creating a self-sustaining team. True residual income requires people who can run their own businesses without you. Having 1,000 people on that Zoom call is great for our ego, having 10 leaders running their own 100 people Zooms is great for our freedom.

Once identified, these leaders need to go into a separate room, because they don't duplicate. They are individuals, they require 1:1 mentorship. It is essential to their success and yours. It's essential to identify the correct people to ensure your 1:1 time is spent with the people who deserve it. Your general team can be trained through systems, your leaders require individual mentorship.

This is where we need to slow down for a moment in order to go faster later. In order to effectively train the leaders on how to lead, we have to ensure that we've done the work ourselves. We need to learn the skills in order to teach the skills. We can borrow and follow other people's systems at the start. But if you want to train leaders, you need to go through the process of creating your own, so that you can teach them how to do the same. It's not 'duplication', it's 'reproduction'.

As much as we want to sprint to the end of the journey, full throttle the whole way – we have to dedicate time to our apprenticeship. We should learn how-to so that we can help our future leaders with the same. They'll use the platform that we create – and go off and do their own thing.

You can make money through the following systems, and you can make good money through promoting systems. Freedom is created by leading yourself and others. But you can't do that without committing to the skills.

Stage 4: Passive Income

The final quadrant is learning how to manage and multiply your money. The money we can earn in this industry is crazy, but nobody ever created freedom by spending all their money. Buying new cars, taking beautiful holidays, and upgrading your home is great, but if you do this too soon, you never truly escape the hamster wheel. It's a bigger wheel, with more expensive toys on it – but if you're making $1 million a year and spending $1 million a year – you're never truly free.

If you're committed to creating a legacy, you must send a percentage of your earnings to work. When you send your money off to work, it generally comes home with more money. Then you can send that money off to work too – and it comes home with even more money. Once your money is off making money, freedom becomes a matter of time.

Coach Rob's Notes: "Creating a 'wealth loop' is a game-changer. By reinvesting a portion of your earnings wisely, you accelerate your journey to financial freedom. Always remember, it's not just about making money, but also about making your money work for you. Build a solid financial strategy and stick to it."

I like to call this a 'wealth loop' – and Network Marketing allows us to hyper-accelerate the process. When I realized we could create an additional income stream that allowed us to 10x, 20x, and 50x our investment budget and have that wealth loop spinning faster - we were off. We started with the end in mind and used Network Marketing to fast-track that journey.

The biggest weakness of passive income is that it requires time to develop. The compound effect is slow at the start. But once that snowball gains momentum and accelerates, let's go! Having both time and money requires you to invest both time and money. You need to be patient while the foundations are being laid.

When we try to 'rush' investments and create our wealth quickly – that generally only comes with a very high level of risk. Risk does not equal reward, risk equals risk. The flip side is that investing is 10% knowledge and 90% patience. Which means that you don't need to overwhelm yourself in the process. Passive income should be exactly that: passive. You can start your investment journey alongside your Network Marketing journey. Start with small amounts and progressively increase your contributions as your business grows.

You can concurrently build your business and legacy – enjoying more freedom now and a more significant legacy later. Developing a simple and reliable, strategy – and then letting it compound behind the scenes while you're building your business. You don't need to be a Wall Street genius; you just need to start with the end in mind. Set your financial goals and have a crystal-clear destination. Take the time to work out what you want, now and in the future – then set your GPS and don't lose focus.

Commit to the learning, commit to the journey, and commit to the work. You'll be able to inspire thousands along the way, and they'll be able to follow the roadmap you've just created for them.

*"In our world,
the sky isn't even the limit."*

— Alpha Femme

BRENDA GEIGER

- Multiple 6 figure earner.

- Former beauty professional helping others in the industry stop exchanging time for money.

- Non-Profit President and Founder.

- Created multiple social media communities with over thousands of women.

- Currently working with award winning international sale high level performance coach.

- Founder of Unbecoming Beta brand.

Let's start out this chapter with some vulnerable honesty. I have barely written more than a Facebook status in the last ten years. Yet here I am as a co-author of a network marketing book with other powerhouses in the industry. Self-doubt has definitely reared its ugly head, and imposter syndrome has set in big time. But, that is no reason to stop or say no when incredible opportunities come our way. I continue to remind myself of the experiences I have had, the incredible accomplishments I have created, and that I absolutely have something to share that will be of value to you.

I am a badass with my craft. I have generated multiple six-figures in the last couple of years without having to step foot into an office or ask for a single day off. I have learned how to utilize and make money using free platforms that are available to all, but so many people don't take advantage of them. I've learned to dance with the changes in the industry and shifted my strategies to complement the evolution of what we know as social media today. In this chapter, I am going to focus on Facebook, but understand the strategies and truths that I share will work with whatever social platform you decide to use for your business.

Congratulations on taking the initiative to be coachable and for investing in yourself! Throughout this book, you will have learned techniques that will help you collapse time so you do not have to fail forward as many times. We, as authors, are here to help accelerate your business goals quicker. As you read this chapter, I want to invite you into my mind and heart and take you behind the scenes of the art of building a social media account that is congruent to your brand.

I want you to think of your social media as your unique fingerprint. It is a social resume of your past and present that will potentially set you up for the future. It can be your virtual connection to loved ones and strangers worldwide. Grab your favorite beverage, get comfortable, and get ready to dig into the science behind one of our most significant business resources.

Coach Rob's Notes: "But don't leaders have it all figured out? They aren't ever scared? Brenda, thanks

for starting out with the vulnerability. I have had multiple conversations with Brenda about her worries with writing her chapter, and you will all be glad she did once you read through it. Just remember that being scared is part of the process to success. Brenda, like all leaders, still has fears, but the greatest difference between her and the unsuccessful is that she is willing to hit those fears head. That example and piece of advice is more important than any skill we will ever learn because if we don't face those fears no amount of skill will ever compensate for our lack of deliberate action."

The Foundation

If you are anything like me, you have probably scrolled back on your own timeline to see what you used to post about. Or maybe you have had one of the notifications come up that says, "Look back four years ago." That is followed by pictures or your posts from four years ago. I remember the day that I first learned how to search my own timeline. I spent a good hour looking back, and one question kept popping into my head, "How in the world did I get here from there?" I couldn't believe that here I was, a six-figure earner that was crushing life, but there I was, reading posts I made in the past that would definitely lead me to have success. I became obsessed with reverse engineering and figuring out what my evolution in the online space had been. I found one key element when I started to investigate my own timeline. The foundation of a great business in your network.

We all have people that we connect with online. Most of those people, in the beginning, are going to be people you personally know. Friends and family, or people that you knew in your past. As you start to use social media more impact-fully, we want to start to think more about our network and why we are connecting with them on social media.

Do we want to keep up with them? Do we want to share our lives and what is going on? Or did we simply hit "accept" when the friend request came through and never thought about them again?

Social media is all about connecting. You can connect with incredible humans and never once be in their physical presence. As I looked back, I realized that the shift for me happened when I started to not just see my network online as just random people that I didn't care about and only knew, sort of. But it completely shifted when I started to take my network seriously and started to care about them.

Eight years ago, my cousin, probably out of pity, and three strangers, interacted with my post on Facebook. The post said, "The traffic on the White Horse Pike sucks." Riveting, I know! If you read that status, how would you feel? Most of you may not know the road or have any experience or feelings about it. Eight years ago, I was not thinking about my network. I was posting small things that weren't impacting anyone at all. What was the objective of this post? What was I hoping to accomplish with it? These are the questions that most people don't ask when they go to post on Facebook or social media.

Your network matters and is essential to building your business. It doesn't matter if they buy from you or become a team member in your business, but you want to think about who you are posting to and why it matters to them. Here are a couple of questions that can help you get more clear about your posts and using social media in a serving way. "Who am I? What are my values? How can I help and serve? How can I make someone feel valid and connected from thousands of miles away? How could I form a relationship so they could feel my truth and intention? What is interesting to me that I can share that will be interesting to them? What solutions am I offering?"

My cousin probably didn't care about the traffic. It was insignificant with no education, call to action or even a funny story. The post was bland and fell flat. If I were to go back and think about my network, I would have created a completely different post. As you build a foundation on social media, start by thinking about your network and how you want to show up for them.

When I went from venting to value, my posts started changing, and I got way more interaction than I did before.

Coach Rob's Notes: "Social media is called social media for a reason. Be social. The network marketers who have the most success on social media have learned how to use it the right way. Brenda summed up best when she said, "Social media is all about connecting. You can connect with incredible humans and never once be in their physical presence."

As I looked back, I realized that the shift for me happened when I started to not just see my network online as just random people that I didn't care about and only knew, sort of. But it completely shifted when I started to take my network seriously and started to care about them."

Many call it fake chit-chat. I look at it completely differently. Yes, you need to guard your time but think of it this way. Just be a good human being. Become a networker first and a network marketer second. Once I discovered how to be a networker first, the doors of success opened for me.

Personal Development

The second place I saw change on my timeline was when I started to take personal development seriously. Listen, I get it; you probably have been told time and time again, but I'm here to tell you that change starts when you start to change internally. I didn't understand the 1% compound rule, but knew that if I showed up a little better and made people feel a little better, more people would connect with me.

I was becoming a product of the law of attraction without realizing it. So ask yourself right now, "What am I doing to change myself internally? How dedicated am I to personal development and doing the work I need to do?"

I started to dig deeper into my own personal development and really started to figure out who I was. The personal development dots started to connect, and I started to create some external changes that aligned with the internal changes I had been working on. Personal development can feel daunting, and I know many people get hung up on where to begin. Let me give you the first step. Start by finishing this book! Then go right out and get *The Game of Networking* by Rob Sperry. These two books are great starting points to your own personal development journey with a paycheck! (If you take it seriously and take action.)

Embody

The third thing I saw that changed over my social media timeline was something I call embodiment. It wasn't until I started walking beside and becoming a true representation of my products that I felt completely aligned with my audience. I couldn't serve my audience when I wasn't using my own products. I couldn't serve my audience if I was using my products and loving them, and not sharing!

When I allowed myself to fall madly in love with the process and actually share about it, I saw myself slowly entering a new playing field. My network watched my life change right before their eyes because I was willing to let them come along and post about it. As I started to embody the change, I noticed that consistency with posting became simple because my daily activities aligned with my mission. I allowed myself a complete lifestyle change to happen. I publicly documented it and brought my network along with me. They didn't have to question if the products worked or if the opportunity provided me with the income; my journey told the story and became all the social proof I needed. My life was in alignment with my opportunity.

The goal was never to lose myself in my brand but to have it become an extension of me. The more I shared, the more my audience flourished, and people became more engaged. My audience was witnessing my growth, and I was showing them how they could do it too. I showed them it was possible and as they watched the blueprint come into fruition. It became just as natural for me to share my opportunity and products as it was to share my children's achievements. Consistency, transparency, and integrations are the formula to success on social media.

Your Next Steps

So what are your next steps? First, I want you to do your own investigation on your personal timeline. What do you post about? How are you showing up on social media? Cultivating connection is key. In order to do that, we want to first know how you are doing. It's not a problem if you find yourself lacking in this department. That's why you are here!

Once you have taken a look at your own timeline, decide what you want to change in order to create value and connection with your network. It can be a commitment to one or two simple steps. You can share more tips, stop complaining so much, or even start commenting back when someone leaves you a comment. Pick a couple of things and stick with them.

Next, I want you to think about how you are responding, reacting, and interacting with your audience on their timelines and DMs (direct messages). Most people tend to miss out on some of the most important aspects of social media. The connection! I once listened to training, and he said that the crucial times to connect with people are in moments of celebration and sorrow. I had never connected the importance when it came to building a solid connection, but people are posting celebrations and sorrows on social media because they are seeking connection from their network.

I'll give you an example. If a beloved pet has been lost, there are usually hundreds of people that express their condolences in the comment section. But how many people actually take the initiative to give that grieving friend time and validation of their loss in the DMs, or even better, in person. Connection means that we are taking the next step. We are sending a private message, creating a voice clip, or picking up the phone and giving them a call. Lasting impact is created during these times because people are asking for connection, and it will be remembered.

The last step that I want to share with you is simple but it can be the most challenging when starting a business. Be human. You can connect with people in genuine ways while sharing your opportunity or product. Remember that everyone is struggling with something and that everyone is craving connection. Lock eyes with people, take a step above the minimum when you are interacting online, and always think about how you can support other people through your posts. You can truly make a lasting impact on someone and never meet them in person!

Coach Rob's Notes: "Your social media is your brand. Do not overcomplicate it but make sure you pay attention to it. Be deliberate on the consistent themes you talk about. Who are you? How can you help others get to know you better in an authentic way? I still say the greatest compliment I receive pertaining to social media is when I first meet someone in person, and they tell me that they already feel like they know me. That's the power of social media done right!"

"It's totally possible for you to design and live an extraordinary life."

– Darren Hardy

BRITT AND MATT RIDDELL

Matt

- Began as a customer for 2 years.

- Recruited 38 people in his first 90 days.

- Went full- time in 2012 and has been with one company for 19 years.

- First Gen Y Diamond in company history.

- Company advisory board member.

- Eleven-time annual conference and leadership keynote speaker.

- Driven by helping people step up and live their best life.

Britt

- Has built 2 six figure businesses in 8 years.

- One of the youngest multiple six figures Elites in company history.

- Company product innovation advisory board member.

- Annual conference and industry event speaker.

- Multiple incentive trip winner.

- Fiercely passionate about helping people discover network marketing.

On How We Got Started

Matt & Britt

When we both reflect back, it's almost like we didn't choose network marketing - it chose us.

Neither of us were specifically looking for a network marketing business, but we were definitely looking for what it offers - a better way to do life. We each wanted more options, more freedom and exciting income potential.

Matt

I totally believe that for anyone with an entrepreneurial spirit, network marketing is the ultimate business vehicle. Why? One word. Leverage. Very few employees actually appreciate how powerful this concept is. What's leverage? Put simply, it's the power of people. What sets our industry apart from everything else is that you, as a business owner, can recruit other business owners - and if you're a leader, you can grow an amazing organization. As a young entrepreneur, I had my first business by the age of 22, and after two years of traditional hiring and firing, I just knew there had to be a better way. Hence, the reason I was so drawn to investigating what network marketing had to offer. It was a combination of frustration and inspiration. Frustrated at trying to get ahead in small business, and inspired by people I was meeting who were literally living the dream through network marketing. I didn't say yes right away because I had other commitments, but when the time was right and I made my decision, it was like a switch got flicked. Within the first four years I broke every record in the company history and became the youngest diamond ever. There's a lesson there - keep in touch with people. Imagine if my sponsor had given up because I said no at the start. Keep a vision and see what's possible for people - that's real leadership.

Britt

I bleed network marketing. I was born into the industry and when I was growing up, it was normal to talk about goals and dreams and going after what you wanted in life. Mum and dad probably didn't realize that by saying yes to network marketing just how impactful their decision would really be for me. I was watching their every move and example. Children are so perceptive and take on everything you do and say. I believe leadership starts at home, and I encourage anyone who is involved in this industry to get your kids involved, too. I adopted their work ethic just because they were leading by example. My parents taught me that I really could be or do anything I want in life. They taught me to dream and they gave me a taste of what the industry promise is all about. Every night when mum and dad would tuck me into bed, they would ask me the same question, and they would answer it in the same way. They would ask me, "Britt, what do you want to do or be when you grow up?"

I had no clue I was five years old. But they would tell me, "Britt, you can be anything you want to be, and you can do anything you want to do if you put your heart to it". That affirmation stuck.

That little girl grew up believing just that. This is the magic part of this industry that I would like to highlight! Most people are walking around out there not realizing their full potential, because somebody didn't give them permission to dream BIG or tell them that they actually can achieve it or give them a game plan on how to do that. Talk to your kids about dreams, goals, and fill those little dear hearts up with endless possibilities. It really does start here first. You are changing the world through your children, too. This is where your legacy begins.

So naturally, by having entrepreneurial parents and knowing that other options existed, I didn't want to work the forty-five year plan, I didn't want to be told what I was worth (per hour) and I didn't want to be ruled by an alarm clock. I wanted a lifestyle that I could fall in love with, and I knew this industry was real!

When I was old enough I "dabbled" in a few different companies, trying to figure it out and find my feet. I actually decided that network marketing wasn't for me at that time and I may review it later. Looking back now with more experienced eyes, I wasn't given a road map, a real method for duplication with a proven system for anyone to win at. I needed leadership, I also had to grow, and everything is always timing. Despite my enthusiasm and belief in the industry, I was slightly disheartened at my first experience because I didn't know what I was doing and I needed guidance and so I parked network marketing on the side. It wasn't until my dearest girlfriend Hannah, who was just a raving fan customer (not a business builder), invited me along to a wine and cheese overview night where I met my now husband Matthew. Hannah who was advocating passionately about products she had discovered really got my interest. I thought it was fascinating that a customer was promoting a business event, and I thought "wow, they must have nailed customer culture," and this concept had my attention. I didn't dive in straight away, I wanted to make sure this was the "one." In fact, Matt had outstanding follow up, and kept inviting me to the next thing - both two important principles with network marketing that everyone should implement ASAP in their business. Together we now have a global multi-million-dollar business, and I wouldn't change it for anything. I absolutely love what I do, and I love the fact that I met Matt through networking!

On What Works

Matt + Britt

We have seen so many patterns emerge of what works, and what doesn't work in network marketing. One of the biggest gaps we see in network marketing is that people sign others up and don't take them on the growth journey.

They just sign them up and say, "Off you go." You must be invested in the development of your newest people. This isn't a business that is a "one and done". You have to create systems that support the development of others. We have set up a system that tells them exactly what the next step is. Once they accomplish that, they move onto the next step. It is simple. Otherwise, people don't know what to do.

Coach Rob's Notes: "Not only do Matt and Britt have amazing Aussie accents but they are incredible leaders that give a very unique perspective. Each one of them spoke at an event I hosted in Australia. I was impressed with their ability to break things down and simplify complex ideas. They understand the value of systems to create a long lasting business. Part of creating great systems is focusing on the development of your team. This section will be a next level type section to give you a vision of what you want and need in order to take your business to the highest ranks."

Matt

You will come across laser focused entrepreneurs who just join and crush it, but lots of people take time. For example, when I first got started, you could buy a business in a bag for about $400. It had a system handbook, a bunch of books, CD's and a few DVD's, and was literally the best $400 I ever invested. I sponsored thirty-eight people in ninety days and the rest is history. That said, it's important to remember that a majority of people who join us don't have business experience, so making sure that the tools and frameworks exist so that anyone can learn at their own pace and grow into leadership is critical. Spend your time working with leaders, but be there for everyone and have the support systems in place so everyone can win.

Britt

It's true! People need to be guided. They are diving into something that is new and with new comes fears and limiting beliefs. These feelings are only natural and with a duplicatable system with simple steps partnered with action, coach-ability and a support team your newest person will be well on their way to personal growth and business growth!

If you are teaching someone to drive a car, you don't tell them everything at once. You teach them what to do, one thing at a time and you show them. People learn by doing, with someone in the co-pilot seat. Just like driving. The temptation is to take over and do it for them, but they will never learn.

The best thing is let them do it averagely and be there with them encouraging and directing. With practice, they will get better and better, courage will turn into competence and competence will turn into confidence. Watching people grow is the best part of what we do. With access to endless information, there are so many different things available. You have so many "industry experts" coaching in this space, particularly with social media and for someone new, it can be very overwhelming. Even people who want to be big influencers using social media have to start with a simple first step process so that it can be duplicated down the line. I have a love / hate relationship with social media as I would rather have leaders than followers as an influencer. What you do must always be duplicatable and simple for the newest person to implement and get results.

On Systems

Matt

Bruce Lee said, "I don't fear a man that has done 10,000 kicks once, I fear the man that has done one kick 10,000 times." That is getting in and learning the skills. Think about someone going to University. What happens if you go two of the three years. You don't get your degree. Same thing here. A typical MBA takes eight years. You can earn an MBA in this business as well. If you invested your time, energy, and growth into this business for eight years, and do it, you don't leave with a piece of paper - you come out with a Massive Bank Account.

Now, at the time of this book we are at a crossroads of new meets old, offline meets online, and there is a lot of confusion as to 'what works' and following systems. Especially for people like me! If you're over 35 and you've been in network marketing for more than a decade, you'll know exactly what I mean.

Here's my take on it. The one thing that doesn't change is the fact that we are a relationship business. Period. The forms of connection and communication we use have evolved, and as leaders we need to make sure our systems are constantly evolving to meet the changing way people communicate with each other.

Britt

We use Facebook groups as a hub for new prospects and we use the Boards app to teach team members on how to do the business. I am sure this will change as the way to do business evolves. Right from the start, we are aiming to get new recruits into momentum. We are launching people, not joining people. We give them exact directions.

Give people the exact next step; just like we mentioned before. We blend the traditional principles with what's relevant now. We have them do a curiosity post (with ideas already mapped out for them) on social media as it's an easy way to share an experience and it's an indirect way to see who is looking for what you have got. We have them make a ten best and ten easiest list. Who are your ten best people that you would like to recruit into your team? Who are the ten easiest people to recruit to your team?

Helping them reach out and start conversations and invite is really important. Connection equals relationships and relationships equal business. We help and guide them through that. We also leverage the three-way messenger chat and help them through this. This is new, and you may need to hold their hand and guide them. In the beginning I teach them to be a really good connector while they have their training wheels on. That way, they can be guided while they are creating their new business muscle.

For as far as training goes, create a system, follow it, and make it easy to use. Maybe your upline or sponsor has something already in place. Don't reinvent it. Get into the system and use it! You have to have it so easy that someone that is ready to go can go through your training on a weekend. Because they will do it. Winners are going to win. You need to have room for your rockstar, or they will find someone else to win with.

Matt

Thanks to social media, no leader, no matter how successful you have been in the past, can rest on yesterday's achievements. The world is so much more transparent and you need to constantly keep learning and stay in the field practicing to remain relevant. Lucky for us, this is the most fun and rewarding profession there is, especially if it's done in an authentic, natural way. We live in a time of rapid evolution. What worked last year in social media might not be applicable now. I remember when Facebook live was THE way in 2015 (TikTok didn't even exist yet!). The people who are crushing it in the industry today have two things in common, in my opinion. They are highly adaptable, and they have a relentless work ethic.

Britt

For us, we literally do business as we do life, and we totally love it. It's all about changing people's lives. While there are so many ways to build a business with social media, there is nothing more simple than just reaching out to someone and seeing how you can serve them with what you have to offer.

Coach Rob's Notes: "When people join your business, they aren't just joining the business. They are joining YOU. They are joining a team. They are joining a system. Why do so many people buy franchises? They want a system. This gives them direction. People want a plan. People want some sort of security. People want proof of a system. Matt and Britt get this so well. They understand the value of following a simple system. If your team has one, then follow it. If your team doesn't have one and you are overwhelmed, then start small and follow the guidelines from this section."

Become System Dependent Not Leader Dependent

Matt

Confession. My business was very "Matt dependent" for a long time. You can figure out if your business is only about you if you are getting all of your volume from your first four levels. It is difficult to take it lower than that if the business is built on you. When your business becomes system dependent, it will build like crazy. It literally explodes. For lots of people - me included - this is the shift that will take you from struggle to success, from frustration to inspiration. It's the true game changer for your business.

Britt

We are super system driven, and obsessed by making it fun, simple, easy, and duplicatable. And if you do it right, it's magical. People can join your business, up-skill themselves, and be winning super quick.

Create A Raving Fan Culture

Matt + Britt

One of the most valuable things we do is create our own team culture and customer culture. We love our company. We love the culture, but it can change. Companies change all the time, and we really have to invest in what we can control. We are fully in control of our team culture and customer culture.

We drive the team culture. We create a super strong product culture, and we don't lose when we focus on the product. The customer culture is huge. You have to be passionate and live and breathe what you are doing. It is hard to do something if you aren't passionate about what you are doing. Think for yourself about how you are going to create a customer and team culture from the beginning. It doesn't have to be elaborate. Just think about how you will treat your customers. Think about what type of team you want to have and cultivate. It can be easy with simple things done consistently. Our philosophy is simple - aim to create raving fans. Not only do they become your most dedicated, loyal, loud customers, they'll often be your best recruits!

On Commitment

Matt

Be before you are and you will become. If you want to have a huge team, then act like it today. Be consistent and act the part. I can only give what I know works. When I started my personal training studio in 2004, I remember sitting there with a document for a $55k loan. I told myself, "If I sign this, I am all in." There was no backing out. I signed the loan docs and got to work. I treated this business exactly the same from the first day. I signed that application form, and got to work.

Make the decision to do network marketing and stick with it for a minimum of five years. If you don't have the skills it doesn't matter, you have time to learn. It doesn't matter what other people are doing, start where you are and commit to being all in for five years. Make a decision and show up for five years, and show up like you have $55k on the line.

Britt

It is a decision to be a leader. It's not something that is given, it's taken. You are a part of something bigger than you when you decide to lead. Leading is showing up and being an example for others. You don't need to have a team (yet) to lead. It's about implementing leadership principles as soon as you get started. Commitment and leadership go hand in hand in my opinion. Whatever you decide to do with your life, you have to be all in. You have to have a decided heart. You have to not just do the things, but decide in your heart that you are all in.

Energy is everything, and your heart is at the hub of it. "I love to see people grow, like our introverts on our team, because they have made a commitment to their future self." What people transform into is so gratifying, and most people surprise themselves as they level up, kick goals, grow, contribute and conquer! Just remember, it all starts with commitment. There have been plenty of occasions where the team has been committed to a particular outcome (maybe a new rank title as an example) and sometimes the outcome can feel as though it is not in reach but because we are committed to making things happen, we double down as a team with activity and things can move very fast with intention. Leadership is two things. Sacrifice and service. As soon as you decide to sacrifice, to go above and beyond and serve others, you are a leader.

On What Is Working Right Now

Matt

Be willing to see what is relevant now and adjust to it. There was a fixed system for twenty years. What happened was the internet came and changed everything, especially with social media. It comes to getting products in people's hands. Doesn't matter how you do it.

Britt

It totally comes down to conversations. You can create content on social media all day long, but it really is how willing you are to have conversations - whether it be online or offline. Connect, invite, and offer.

Content might be king, but conversation is queen. By getting to know someone, you really can discover how best you can serve them. How can you change that person's life through what this industry has to offer? Think about walking into a pub and sitting next to someone on a stool.

You can say all of your amazing content and it would be weird. They would probably move, or worse! You have to start a conversation. People don't care about your content unless they see that you are interested in them. Add value! Start a conversation. Start a simple conversation.

Care. Be interested in others while everyone else is focused on being interesting! It gives you a tremendous advantage. Frazer Brooks uses LORD (location, occupation, recreation, and dreams and desires). Do this, and you will know that person better than half of their friends - and as we know, people do business with people they know, like and trust.

The Power Of Events

Matt + Britt

For us, events have been the key to business growth. 100 percent. Leaders are born at events. Decisions are made at events. Lives are changed at events. From a recruiting prospective, we build our business from event to event.

Matt

I got recruited because my sponsors invited me to an event. In fact, I went to four of them before I made a decision! The event does the work for you, you just have to invite people. It also gives our team an actionable step to take for the week. We tell them, their job is to invite people to this one event for the week.

Here are the magic words for the invite, "Hey listen, there is an event on such and such a date and I thought you might want to know about it because...." And then you fill in the blanks because you know that person. I never randomly invite someone to an event until I have a relationship and know how I can serve them.

Britt

It is always evolving. Our mentors always taught us, always have events! It is key. In fact, that is how I was introduced by my dear friend Hannah. It doesn't matter if it is in person or online. As we said, leaders are born at events. Want more leaders? Have more events. We do Monday night training. Ninety percent of our team is on these calls because we keep it short and sweet, usually thirty minutes. We always give them the action item for the week, as well.

I think the biggest thing that holds people back in network marketing is their hesitation with the unknown. They are doing something they have never done and going someplace they have never been. So naturally your brain tries to protect you and tell you it is scary. It is actually nature taking over here. It's instinct and has been happening for millions of years to protect our species from danger. You must overcome that. Action cures fear.

The Magic Belief - It's Not About You

It's all about making a difference. We have shared some of our top ways to keep your business thriving and not making it all about you. This business is about people. The more you can go out and help people succeed, the more your business thrives. We always say that your bonus each month shows how many people you helped that month. Watch your wealth grow as you help people grow. Make it simple on yourself by creating systems that work for you, and always be willing to grow with the team culture leading the way.

With how big the online world is becoming, many are forgetting the importance of events. Social media can enhance your lead generation and sponsoring events still create that necessary bond and camaraderie. As they mentioned, "leaders are born at events." Whenever your company or team has a large event, promoting that event should become your main focus. One of the best ways to amplify your efforts is to have as many team members as possible at those big events.

There is a magic to them that can't be explained. It is one of the top ways I build my business, and nothing will ever replace that feeling of a big event. Trust us and focus on the big events!

Coach Rob's Notes: "As mentioned by Britt and Matt, social media is incredible but it means nothing if you aren't having those daily conversations. I cannot stress this enough. There is no secret strategy that teaches you to avoid having those daily conversations. You still need to have those and focus on them daily. That is why The Network Marketing strategy planner/tracker is so needed. What we track and measure grows."

"I do what others won't so I can experience things others don't!"

— Burke Green

BURKE GREEN

- Boasts over three decades of unparalleled success and leadership in the Network Marketing industry, achieving the highest pin level in three separate companies.

- As a founding distributor of two prosperous ventures, Burke has played a pivotal role in their ascent to success, cultivating organizations with over 1 million distributors.

- Burke's organizations have generated over $20 billion in sales and more than a billion dollars in commissions, showcasing his knack for fostering thriving business ecosystems globally, spanning 60 countries.

- Recognized as one of the industry's most sought-after trainers, Burke's innovative (How To) training system reflects his dedication to equipping distributors with skills for success.

- Beyond leadership and training, Burke is an authority on compensation plans, leveraging over three decades of experience to optimize earnings for himself and his teams.

Mastering The Game You Are Playing

Coach Rob's Notes: "Burke Green's journey from a farm in Wyoming to becoming a sage in the network marketing industry underscores a vital lesson: Understanding the game you're playing is crucial. His basketball anecdote isn't just a humorous tale; it's a powerful metaphor for the importance of knowing the rules of your chosen field. In network marketing, this translates to grasping the nuances of the compensation model and the industry's dynamics. Burke's insights highlight the criticality of preparation, research, and commitment in succeeding in network marketing. His story and subsequent success serve as an invaluable blueprint for those aspiring to make their mark in this competitive landscape. Pay attention to Burke's wisdom— his experience and understanding of the game's "rules" offer a roadmap to mastering network marketing."

To win in any game, it's crucial to understand the rules. If you're reading this book or immersing yourself in this industry, and particularly if you're associated with Rob Sperry, I feel that it is safe to make a couple of assumptions. First, it's likely that you are curious about network marketing as a career, or at the very least you aspire to generate substantial income - transforming it into a viable side hustle. I would like to share with you a few things that I have learned about the network marketing game from many years of experience in this industry. To truly thrive and be a real player, you must understand the rules of the game you're playing. Before we dive in, I would like to share a story with you.

My name is Burke Green. I grew up on a farm in Alta, Wyoming, which is a little rural community on the western side of the Tetons from Jackson Hole. There were thirty of us kids in my grade school. That's grades one through six, and we didn't have organized sports. After grade school, I went to middle school in Driggs, Idaho. This was before the NBA youth programs such as Junior Jazz were really big. I had a lot of experience playing basketball on the playground and I loved all sports. I especially loved contact sports like football. I was a pretty big kid for my age and was also pretty athletic, so I tried out for the basketball team in seventh grade. The time came for our very first game. I was excited to play! I wasn't a starter in the game, but for some reason, the coach decided to throw me into the mix. This is where it gets good.

When the coach put me in the game, I ran down the court to set up the defense. As I previously shared, I was pretty big for my age and, growing up with big brothers, I was kind of the rough and tumble type. As I stood under the basket, the point guard from the other team came down the court, and drove the middle lane towards me. I had just finished the football season playing middle linebacker when I started basketball. When he came driving in at full speed I thought, there's no way this little dude is going to score on me.

I basically went up with my full body and blocked him as he tried to make a shot! In the process of blocking him, I knocked him down. For reasons that are obvious to me now, but weren't then, the shooting foul was called on me. This was the first play of my basketball career. Everybody lined up on the foul line while the opposing player was setting up to shoot. Just before he shot the ball I heard the coach yell "Burke, get the ball." So I thought, Okay, let's go. Well, he missed the first shot and the ball bounced off the rim to the other side of the court. I can't exactly remember how it happened, but I ended up with the ball and there were several opposing team members laying on the ground. The whistle blew and guess what? I got called for another foul. Now we were in the penalty so it was a one and one situation on the foul shots.

Again we lined up. I got ready. They shot the ball. They missed the ball and I got the rebound again. If I'm anything, I'm consistent. Again there were players from the opposing team on the ground. At this point I was very confused as to why the ref kept calling fouls on me. I got the ball, wasn't that the goal? This same scenario happened four times in a row. Opposing team would shoot the foul shot, he would miss, I got the rebound and a couple of people ended up on the floor. My very first organized game of basketball ended up with me fouling out of the game with five fouls in less than one minute of play. After that first foul, the opposing team never left the foul line until I fouled out.

I came off the court confused and pretty frustrated. I felt that I had done what was asked of me. I got the ball. I expressed this to my coach who was chuckling as I came over to him.

Coach said, "Burke, sit down. We've got to have a talk about what was happening. I love the effort and enthusiasm, but you need to learn the rules of the game."

I didn't understand the rules of the game that I was playing. I was playing football on the basketball court, and because I didn't understand the rules, I was penalized and basically taken out of the game very quickly. In less than one minute, I received five fouls and had to sit on the bench for the rest of the game. That is how my basketball career started.

What does that story have to do with our industry? I'd like to make some comparisons. I was taught and I think many of us were, that we should go to high school to get good grades, so we can go to college. We then go to college to get good grades to get a good job. When we do all that, then we do the research, preparation and we go through the process of getting a job. We do all the different things. Then when we sit down. In our first job interview, we went through the process. Our boss gives us the definition of the job description. We go to work and we negotiate our salary, then we go to work.

We do all those things! Well, in this industry, in the direct sales industry, the network marketing industry, typically a friend calls us, or we answer a Facebook post or something like that. Then we join the business. We enter this industry with the mindset of trying it for ninety days and see how it goes, and if we're not making X amount of money or if the product isn't exactly what we think it should be, we move on to the next company. Even though we have not given it the time to grow or the effort to make it happen we move on. What would happen if we did that in our careers?

Now, here's the thing that's crazy to me. When I see people do this, and I've been doing this for thirty three years, it absolutely astounds me how people enter this business and they say, "Oh, my gosh! I joined this business, I joined this industry, and I am going to get rich!" With no forethought, with no thinking about it, with no study, no research, none of those things.

I have a couple of questions that I want to ask you, and I want you to think about this now. I travel all over the world doing trainings, meetings, doing those sorts of things, and I always ask these two questions:

The first question, and I want you to think about this is, how many of you before today have been involved, exposed, or seen another network marketing company or direct sales company?

When I ask that question, it doesn't matter where in the world I am. At this point every single hand goes up. At this point in the world everyone has been exposed or involved in this industry.

When I ask the next question, and that is how many of you had a good experience or actually made money with your previous company? Guess what happens? Probably less than 10% of the hands go up now. The crazy part about that is as I go around and I'm talking to people,

I talk to them about the compensation model. That's basically what we're going to be talking about today is understanding the game and rules and game that you're playing. That's the compensation model. How do we get paid? Okay, we don't just sign up and all of a sudden money starts rolling in. This is a very competitive industry at this point. Just like in any industry, those that are the talented and the most educated usually have a better shot at winning. But, understanding the rules of the game is essential.

There are essentially five different compensation models.

1. There's a stair-step breakaway

2. There's a matrix

3. There's unilevel and binary

4. Then there's a hybrid binary compensation model

5. Hybrid compensation model

Now, when people talk about those different models. That is literally how we get paid in this industry. When we sell a product, there's a commission derived, and that's how we are paid. Well again, let me ask a question. Do you know the nuances of each one of these compensation models? Do you know how to maximize or get the most commissions possible out of each one of these compensation models, or do you just join a company? Hope and for the best, and I've even heard top distributors of companies go. For some, they don't really understand how the compensation plan works. They just want to work and the checks just started rolling in. They just signed up and, gosh, I did this, and money started coming in. Well, guys, that's ridiculous. If you're looking at creating a long-term residual income. You need to understand the game that you're playing.

If you don't, you will be like me in my basketball game, where you will be disappointed and out of the game, or you will be penalized before you even get started, and it'll be very short lived, and then it won't be a good experience, and you'll move on to the next company. Over and over again. Do you know the nuances of their compensation model that would lead you to the next level of income?

When you make a decision to join a company. Is that a product based decision? Is that a compensation model-based decision? Or is it just your friend joins? So you're going to join them, and it's gonna be a fun ride.

If you're looking to create income with this industry, you need to become better at getting involved in the compensation model. Each model has its own nuances. Each model has its good, bad, and ugly. But the biggest thing that I see in this industry is that the vast majority of people don't have any idea, really, how the compensation model works. They don't have any idea how the compensation model actually pays out, how it calculates commissions and how the best way to maximize those commissions are.

Coach Rob's Notes: "Burke Green's basketball story underscores a key lesson for network marketing: The importance of understanding your company's compensation plan. Just like knowing the rules of basketball prevents fouls, understanding the nuances of your compensation model is essential for success. Whether it's a stair-step, matrix, unilevel, binary, or hybrid, each plan has its unique advantages and strategies for maximizing earnings. Burke emphasizes that success isn't about luck but about informed, strategic action. This insight is crucial for anyone serious about making a significant income in network marketing."

So here's my suggestion; When you get involved in a company, you need to understand and do the research necessary to make a smart decision for your future. You need to study. You need to read books. You need to talk to mentors who are doing what you want to do. If you want to make $5,000 a month. Talk to somebody making $5,000 a month. If you want to make $10,000 a month, talk to someone making $10,000 a month. If you want to make $100,000 a month, talk to someone making $100,000 a month. It doesn't matter really what the number is, because this industry will allow you to create any income that you want. But one thing you need to understand is you need to grow as an individual to that level of income just because you joined a company and you joined the network marketing industry that does not give you the God-given right to make $10,000 a month. What are people doing today to make $10,000 a month in this industry? They have studied and learned and grown into that person that is qualified to make that sort of income.

You know this is a competitive industry. When you talk to someone. Do you know the difference between a stair step breakaway and a unilevel and a matrix and a binary? Can you tell them the difference? Or are you just hoping for the best, you? Oh, we got this cool, cool product.

Guess what?

Every company has a cool product. Every company has a viable product, that if people use it, take it, do whatever they need to do with it, they probably derive benefit. In my opinion. The compensation model is one of the biggest issues that people overlook when trying to create an income and trying to create a career in this industry. So if you don't know what your compensation model is or how it works or you're not quite sure-you don't know the rules of the game.

Do you have a strategy to maximize the compensation plan? When I sign someone up I have 3 goals :

1. I want to get them on the product for the benefits they're going to receive.

2. I want to help them make enough money to get their products paid for.

3. I want to move them into profitability.

Do you know how to do that? Do you know what the break-even point is in your compensation model? You know, if people are on a $150 or a $250 a month auto ship. What is it going to take to make $150 to $250 dollars a month? How many people do you have to recruit? How many people have to be on an auto ship? Do you know the numbers?

The next step? Do you know the numbers to help move them into profitability? Do you know what it takes to actually rank up and do the volume? If you don't do that, you're fooling yourselves as far as going out and creating a career in this industry.

So here's my advice: When you look at a compensation model, you need to be able to understand how it pays out. Get with a competent and upline or competent person you know. I've done a lot of consulting around the industry. It's astounding to me how many executives of companies and how many owners of companies don't even know how the compensation models will work, other than, that is what some consultant told them it was a great model, and that sort of thing. They don't know the requirements that it takes. They don't know the different nuances of how their compensation plan works. Get with a confident upline or with a competent person who understands the industry, who understands the models and set up a strategy and a game plan to:

1. Get people to buy your product.

2. Help them get that product paid for.

3. Help you people move into profitability.

From that point on, once they're profitable. The next thing we need to do is help them replace their income from their current job or current career, so they can become a full time member of your team. So with that, hopefully, this has been helpful. See you at the top!

Coach Rob's Notes: "Burke's advice is important for anyone looking to master network marketing. It's all about understanding the game you're playing— knowing your compensation plan inside out. Just joining a company doesn't entitle anyone to earn big; it's about growing into the person who can. This means studying, learning from those already successful, and having a clear strategy. Burke outlines a brilliant approach: Get people loving your product, help them cover their costs, then guide them into making a profit. Knowing the nuances of your compensation model and having a plan to maximize it are key steps often overlooked. His emphasis on being informed, having a strategy for growth, and understanding how to navigate the compensation plan to achieve success is invaluable advice. This is the blueprint for turning aspirations into achievements in network marketing."

"Success is not achieved through dwelling on or avoiding failures, but instead rising every time we fall and persisting with unwavering consistency until we stand as the conqueror of what we set out to achieve."

– Author Unknown

DANA DELORENZO

- Liver Transplant Survivor (2020).

- Division One Collegiate Soccer Player (shout out to Quinnipiac!).

- NASM and AAFA certified fitness trainer.

- First time network marketer.

- Top 0.49% of current company with downline of approximately 100.

Finding Consistency in the Most Challenging Way

In 2019, I found myself grappling with the sudden onset of liver disease, a relentless challenge that gained momentum in the blink of an eye. By December of that horrific year, I received a grim prognosis; having just one month left to live with four young children at home and a life that still needed to be lived. Amidst the whirlwind of uncertainty, consistency became the only anchor in my fragile world, but it was a difficult concept to adopt given my situation.

Fast-forward to January 2020 – An angel donor lost his life in order to grant me the greatest gift a person could receive; LIFE. Miraculously, a life-saving transplant breathed renewed hope into my existence. However, the journey to recovery was no less grueling. Repeated cardiac arrests, collapsed lungs, and having been plunged into a month-long coma, I emerged back to life. While still intubated but coherent and facing the daunting tasks of having to learn to walk, talk and even eat real food again.

I suddenly found consistency to be my unwavering friend. The figurative saying, "one foot in front of the other" became literal to me. I didn't start my rehabilitation with a mile walk, but instead simply standing up from my bed on day one. I didn't feel as if I could push myself past that point; the thought was daunting. However, the thought of never playing sports with my kids again, or doing everyday things with them was suddenly even more daunting than pushing myself.

So, I began. Standing at the foot of the bed evolved into taking ten steps forward. Ten steps forward evolved into a lap around the hospital hallway. Finally, a lap around the hospital hallway quickly evolved over four years into becoming a personal trainer, whooping all four of my kids butts at every sport possible again, and getting into possibly the best shape of my life. The climb I had to make seemed so high, but with each small, consistent and deliberate step forward, I consistently got stronger and stronger in a physical and mental sense.

Though there were challenges appearing unconquerable, it was the relentless commitment to consistency that became my guiding light. Through the darkest moments, my consistency propelled me forward, literally one foot in front of the other. It is here that I found my resilience in the face of adversity in my health journey, but also in so many other aspects of life. It was in those trying times that I discovered the unbeatable strength found within the simple act of staying consistent – a force that ultimately triumphed over the odds and propelled me towards healing and a newfound appreciation for life and now, the permanent adaptation of the act of consistency.

Coach Rob's Notes: "Dana's remarkable journey is a testament to the incredible power of consistency. Her story vividly illustrates that our biggest challenges can become our greatest victories through the simple, yet profound, practice of taking one step at a time. Let this be a reminder to us all that consistency is not just about achieving success in the short term but about playing the long game, overcoming adversity, and emerging stronger on the other side. Dana's resilience and unwavering dedication to moving forward, no matter the obstacle, serve as a powerful inspiration for anyone navigating their own challenges, in network marketing or in life."

Network Marketing Found Me at the Most Opportune Time

Fast-forward to April of that very year. A good friend of mine mentioned her new venture and asked me if I wanted to join her in something that she believed was going to be life changing. I haphazardously jumped aboard the journey of network marketing without an idea of which direction to turn; a venture into the unknown for me. I had never been in this unfamiliar space before and it seemed impossible that I would ever succeed. This was all too similar to how I felt just a few months before; in an unfamiliar position, knowing I needed to rely on consistency to propel me forward.

Even with consistency, my beginning days were a bit rough. Today, reflecting on my initial presence on social media brings about a cringe-worthy realization of my past missteps, so as you can imagine I didn't start in the position of leadership; this came over two years later.

In this industry, the path to leadership and success encompasses highs and lows, victories and setbacks, moments of encouragement, and bouts of defeat. Navigating through this maze of challenges, especially in those early days, demanded not just newfound talent and skill that I never had to possess before, but an intense ability to stay consistent and dedicated to the unknown process. This is what separates those who thrive from those who succumb to misconceptions and eventually failure to continue in this industry.

Network marketing is ever changing so it is no wonder why success is not usually instantaneous. It is a journey of being deliberate, and requiring strategic thinking, resilience, and unwavering consistency. Picture it as the craziest roller coaster in the amusement park. The twists and turns are never ending, leaving even the most experienced entrepreneurs wrestling with discouragement more frequently than one might imagine. Yet, it is within these winding turns that a leader's resilience is forged. Climbing to the peaks of success, only to sink into the depths of challenges in the blink of an eye, is the difficult nature of this industry. It gets a person thinking that it is too hard, or it's pointless to try. Embracing these falls, knowing that each one brings an opportunity for exponential success is crucial to understand during these trying times, especially in the beginning.

Some of these falls may be harder than others. Acknowledge that not every day will be a triumph, and not every sales pitch will result in a sale. Embrace the setbacks as learning opportunities instead of failures and view the peaks as milestones on your journey. The ability to experience both successes and failures with calmness and tactfulness is a trait of a consistent and resilient entrepreneur.

Coach Rob's Notes: "Dana's step into network marketing and her journey through the highs and lows shows us the real value of keeping going even when

it's tough. Her story shows us that winning in network marketing, like in life, comes from facing challenges straight on with consistency and not giving up. Dana's path reminds us that the real win in network marketing comes from sticking to it, learning from every tough spot, and getting back up stronger every time."

Overcoming Failures with Consistency

But, how does one maintain consistency in the face of such adversity and keep their tactfulness? Clarity of one's purpose is key. You must know your why in order to gain that consistency. Reminiscing back to my hospital days; I knew my why. My why was clear — to be able to continue being an incredible mother again for my children.

Why did you embark on this direct sales journey, and what fuels your passion? Whatever your purpose is, it becomes the needle on your business compass. During moments of doubt, you must reconnect with your purpose—remind yourself why you started, and let that very reason propel you forward. Keep coming back to it during your times of struggle to regain that resilience.

Resilience is a building block of our consistency. In network marketing, rejection is not just probable but sometimes necessary and guaranteed. The resounding 'no' is not a sign of failure, but instead a stepping stone toward success. I'm sure you have heard something along the lines of, "the more times you hear the word 'no' the closer you are to a 'yes'."

Not everyone will say yes to your product, service or opportunity. Embrace this, and redefine your definition of rejection. Reframe setbacks as opportunities to learn and grow. Habitual consistency and resilience will fortify you against challenges, transforming adversity into a mere ellipsis in your success story; it is the to be continued...

Time Management and How it Assists in Keeping Consistent

Time management is key to maintaining consistency. With numerous tasks and responsibilities competing for your attention, effective time management techniques can make all the difference in staying on track and maximizing productivity. By establishing specific, achievable objectives, you can prioritize your tasks and focus your energy on activities that will yield the greatest results.

One helpful time management strategy is to use alarms and timers to stay organized and on track throughout the day. Set reminders for important online meetings or tasks to ensure that nothing falls through the cracks. Additionally, consider using timers to allocate specific time blocks for different activities. For example, dedicate thirty minutes to responding to messages.

When in the hospital, I made sure my alarm was set for the big tasks and events throughout the day; mostly just waking up, and assuring I am sleeping on time to assure maximum healing. I mean, what else could a mostly immobile person do? I also employed the timer function on my phone. I would allow myself twenty minutes of time via phone with my kids prior to making myself get up to do my physical therapy.

I then learned to limit my time with a lot of activities throughout the day to avoid boredom, and to assure I kept my mind fresh and giving it a change of pace since I was stuck in one room all day for over a month. By breaking your day into manageable segments, you can stay focused and avoid becoming overwhelmed by the sheer volume of tasks. Mastering time management is vital for staying consistent and achieving success in this industry.

DMOs - Strategies for Staying Consistent for Long-Term Success

The impact of consistency is compounded— each act of consistency builds on top of itself. It's the daily, incremental actions that build success over time. The influence of consistency extends to personal development, which is an integral part to maintaining a successful business especially in this industry. We must continuously engage in our personal development, positive habits and daily methods of operation (DMO's), in order for business to grow. Embracing a consistent routine, whether in business, fitness, mindfulness, or education, amplifies the benefits of perseverance. You must develop habits that are aligned with your purpose and end goals. Consider incorporating daily rituals that align with your personal goals with your DMO's and let this be your guiding force.

DMOs play a crucial role in sustaining consistency. DMOs involve strategic planning and execution of specific tasks daily, weekly and even monthly, contributing to long-term success. Identifying and adhering to your DMOs ensures a fool proof approach, minimizing distractions, and optimizing productivity. Here are some of my non-negotiable personal DMOs, specifically pertaining to Facebook as an example, though they are forever evolving:

• Add five new friends.

• Comment on twenty posts from people who are not part of the company and are therefore prospects.

• Interact with twenty social media stories from people who are not part of the company. Make the reactions are well thought out conversation starters (ie. I love those heels! Where did you get them from?! I have to have those!)

• (I call the above, "warming up my audience")

- Post something from one of my content pillars. A content pillar is a topic to focus on in your daily content that your audience will recognize as something that describes your lifestyle and beliefs. For example, motivation is one of my pillars, so each Monday I will post a cute selfie of myself with a motivational post, sometimes taken from a quote that resonates with me.

- After posting, allow the audience to then respond to the post and go back and respond to every single comment. Yes, every single comment. Doing so improves your algorithm and keeps your prospects in your feed and vice versa.

- Post five to ten stories (approximately 80% personal/funny/ entertaining and 20% business related).

- Listen to or read ten to twenty minutes of personal development via books or podcasts each day.

Remember – these are just my basic non-negotiable DMOs, but they change from time to time and this is the minimum I allow myself to do daily. I do not spend more than two hours per day on these, and that is an overestimate.

Coach Rob's Notes: "Dana's journey highlights the power of sticking to your path, even when times get hard. Her story is a lesson for all of us in network marketing: Success comes from knowing why you started and keeping that reason close, especially when facing challenges. Dana shows that being consistent, managing your time well, and following a daily plan can turn tough situations into growth opportunities. Let her story inspire you to keep going, no matter what, and remember that your daily actions are the steps to your success. Your 'why' is your strength, and your routine is your roadmap to achieving your dreams."

Using Habit Stacking to Assist in Keeping Consistent

Repeated actions shape your mindset, and with practice become habitual. Consistency is not just a set of actions; it is a mindset that transforms challenges into automated building blocks. Nurture mental resilience and consistency by stacking the positive habits that you already possess with those that you are looking to add to your life, whether business related or personal.

Habit stacking is a powerful technique that involves linking new habits to existing ones to create a routine. By piggybacking on already existent behaviors, it becomes easier to integrate and maintain new desired habits. This enhances consistency overtime without having to over-think the planning of things, but instead to automate the positive habits you're seeking.

When I was hospitalized and woke up from my coma, there wasn't much I looked forward to. Being that my vocal chords were torn, I couldn't physically speak with my kids, but my family and friends visiting were able to Facetime them so they could at least talk to me. This was the one thing that I looked forward to the most every morning. I began to make a mental contract with myself; after someone called my children for me and I was able to hear from them for twenty minutes, I would be assisted out of the bed, and I would force myself to do my daily steps to get my muscle memory back and begin to walk again. I would then sit back in bed and do my daily breathing exercises to strengthen my vocal chords and respiratory system so I could talk and eat real food again. Knowing I would talk to my kids again later that night pushed me to get my nighttime physical therapy in as well.

Boom! This is where my habit stacking really began!

To use this in your business life, think of something you do daily that you genuinely enjoy and stack something after it that you might not want to do. "After I allow myself a delicious, hot cup of coffee, I will comment on ten prospects' posts." You can do this with several habits in order to make the act of consistency a simpler task.

Utilizing the Power of Teamwork for Consistency

Maintaining consistency can be challenging on your own at times. Thankfully, no one is ever alone in this industry. Surround yourself with a supportive network. Share experiences, seek advice, learn from other leaders, and offer support in return. Remember that saying, "Your vibe attracts your tribe." Rely on each other to remain consistent – become accountability partners.

By partnering with someone who shares your goals, you can leverage the power of teamwork to stay consistent and achieve your objectives. One effective strategy is to establish an accountability partnership where you and your partner regularly check in with each other to monitor progress and offer support. This mutual accountability fosters a sense of responsibility and motivation, making it harder to slip up or procrastinate.

To take it a step further you can incentivize consistency. Implement a consequence system with your accountability partner. For example, agree upon a consequence – such as paying a small fine – if either of you fails to meet a deadline or fail to remain consistent with given tasks. This adds an extra layer of motivation and consequences for not remaining consistent, making it more likely that you'll stick to your commitments. In the end, you'll either be really broke, or really consistent! No one wants to be broke.

Tying It All Together

Recognize the symbiotic relationship between consistency and adaptability. While consistency provides a stable foundation, adaptability allows you to pivot and evolve in response to changing circumstances in this industry. Merging consistency and adaptability equips you to navigate the unpredictable nature of direct sales with resilience and strategic expertise.

As you progress in your network marketing journey, fine-tune your consistency map. Regularly evaluate and elevate your goals and objectives, ensuring they align with your evolving vision and purpose. Consistency isn't about stubbornly adhering to a single approach but adapting your strategies in response to lessons learned and changing situations. Assess the effectiveness of your habits, routines, and daily modes of operation, refining them to optimize efficiency and effectiveness from time to time.

Start adopting specific strategies for mastering consistency. Explore time-management techniques, explore the benefits of habit stacking, and consider the impact of accountability partnerships. Tailor these strategies to suit your unique style and goals, creating a personalized guide map for consistent success.

Consider the impact of your consistent efforts in the larger picture of your legacy. How you navigate the challenges, celebrate victories, and impart wisdom to those who follow you can become a rewarding experience in itself. People are always watching leaders, and attempting to follow their footsteps. A consistent commitment to growth and resilience sets the stage for a lasting impact on both your immediate team and accountability partners as well as the broader network marketing community/those in other companies. Aspire to leave a legacy that inspires others to embrace consistency as the cornerstone of their success.

Network marketing is not a solitary endeavor; it's about building a community of like-minded individuals striving for success. Consistency is the glue that binds this community together. Actively contribute to the growth of your network, sharing insights, providing support, and celebrating the achievements of your peers. Consistency in fostering a positive and collaborative community amplifies the collective strength, making it an environment where everyone thrives.

Consistency doesn't imply rigidity; it can coexist with innovation and new ways of doing this. New consistencies can be added when practicing the same consistencies overtime. Explore how you can infuse creativity and innovation into your consistent approach. Experiment with new strategies, embrace emerging technologies, and stay attuned to evolving market trends. The synergy between consistency and innovation creates a dynamic force that propels you ahead, ensuring your methods remain relevant and effective.

By integrating all of these facets into your understanding of consistency within the network marketing realm, you not only expand the scope of your business story but also provide a comprehensive guide for new and existing team members seeking success as well. This emphasizes that consistency is not a one-dimensional concept, but it is a dynamic force that is part of every aspect of your professional and personal journey. Network marketing is a marathon, not a sprint. Quick success does not always last, and often has to do with luck – but remaining consistently committed to your goals, regardless of the challenges, is the secret sauce that distinguishes the thriving leaders in the industry from those who dabble and eventually fade out. Embrace consistency as your guiding principle, and let it pave the way for enduring triumphs in your direct sales journey.

"You can have more than you've got because you can become more than you are. Unless you change who you are, you will always have want you've got."

– Jim Rohn

DORA EDMONSON

- Visionary founder of an online membership program at age 62.

- Inspiring Speaker and consultant with 20+ years of experience, while navigating motherhood during spouse's US Navy service.

- Architect of Profitable Solutions for the vacation and Real Estate industries amidst economic challenges.

- Seasoned trainer and mentor specializing in building employee and customer loyalty.

- Emerging entrepreneur thriving in a 40 year marriage, cherished grandmother to seven Grandchildren.

Welcome to the journey of discovering the transformative power of the CARE strategy. For over four decades, I've navigated life's twists and turns armed with a formula that has fostered stability, reliability, and dependability in my relationships with family, friends, and colleagues online and offline.

As a new consultant, I found myself facing a unique challenge when the CEO approached me, intrigued by the rapid transformation I had instigated within his company. In his four-decade career, he had never witnessed such a swift and dramatic shift in company culture and employee loyalty. My initial response was simple: 'I CARE about them.' However, this seemingly straightforward statement led me to profound reflections. What did it truly mean to care about employees? How did I manage to orchestrate this remarkable turnaround in less than 30 days? How did we elevate our customer service ratings from low to high, and our workplace atmosphere from a negative daily grind to an enthusiastic hub of positivity? It was during these introspective moments that I realized the essence of my approach lay in genuinely demonstrating that I cared about every individual within the organization. From that transformative conversation with the CEO, I crafted the CARE formula—a blueprint not only for cultivating robust, productive teams but also for nurturing profound connections with friends and family.

At the heart of the CARE Strategy lie four pillars that build connections and foster understanding.

Commitment to Consistency: The Steadfast Anchor
Attractive Attention: The Magnetic Force
Realistic Responsibility: The Backbone of Dependability
Engaging with Excellence: Elevating Connections with Sincere Support

In a world where the demands of work and family life often pull us in different directions, finding the balance to nurture relationships can be challenging. This is where the CARE Strategy shines, providing a compass to guide us through the intricacies of life. It's a philosophy rooted in the belief that, while we can't always control life's challenges, we can always control our behavior and attitude in response to them.

As you read on, I invite you to reflect on your relationships and consider how the CARE Strategy can bring a new depth and fulfillment to them.

Coach Rob's Notes: "Dora introduces the CARE Strategy, a guide for cultivating meaningful connections in both personal and professional realms. This approach centers on Commitment to Consistency, Attractive Attention, Realistic Responsibility, and Engaging with Excellence. Dora's reflections and experiences underline the importance of genuine care in transforming relationships and organizational culture. As you explore the CARE Strategy, consider how its principles can enhance your interactions and deepen bonds with those around you. As always take notes because Dora always has great content!"

Commitment to Consistency: The Steadfast Anchor

Now, let's dive into the first pillar of the CARE Strategy: Commitment to Consistency.

Steps to living a Commitment to Consistency

- **Prioritize People:** Focus on people over projects. Do you keep a follow-up list to track commitments?

- **Manage My Reactions:** Do I know what triggers me? Do I have a plan to deal with those triggers?

- **Track My Commitments:** Do I document and regularly review promises I made? Am I tracking what I say I will do, and am I doing it when I said I would?

As a 62-year-old grandma venturing into the world of social media, it was my desire to create real friendships online. Being disabled and homebound, I aimed to develop a support system of friends in the digital realm. I recognized the importance of being consistent and positive in building this community of friends. My goal was to stand out and provide value in my posts and support for others. I wanted to be a dependable source of encouragement and assistance for those in my online circle.

To illustrate the importance of Commitment to Consistency, let me share a personal story. As a leader in a social media business, my team was grappling with maintaining consistency in their daily social media tasks. Recognizing their challenges, I was determined to offer guidance and support. To address this issue, I introduced a daily accountability call where team members could gather to focus on their engagement efforts. Every day, I make it a point to be present on that call, ready to roll up my sleeves and work alongside them. This serves as a powerful reminder that they're not alone in their journey and that they have someone readily available to address any questions or concerns.

The journey toward a commitment to consistency isn't a walk in the park. It demands time, effort, and dedication to put these principles into practice. By implementing this daily accountability call, I aimed to not only emphasize the importance of consistency but also provide a tangible means for my team to cultivate this essential trait in their daily routines. Together, we've embarked on this journey, reinforcing the value of reliability and dependability, both in our professional and personal lives.

As a parent of three young children, I came to understand the profound importance of creating a stable home environment. When I was upset, it wasn't just me affected—it had a ripple effect on my children, often spoiling the day for everyone. I yearned to build a positive and stable haven for my kids, a place where they could rely on stability, encouragement, and love. I wanted our home to be their sanctuary, a place where they could find solace from the challenges of the world outside. I realized that while I couldn't control their experiences beyond our home's walls, I could certainly ensure that home was a haven of consistency and dependability. I wanted my children to know that their mom was a steadfast and reliable presence in their lives.

As parents we were interested in the hobbies of our children. I learned to play online computer games so I could join their Friday night dungeon runs. Yes, I am a proud level 64 warrior in World of Warcraft. I participate in the family Fantasy Football leagues and usually take 1st place in the weekly confidence picks. I build worlds with my grandkids in Minecraft and do a pretty good job in Roblox. Believe me it takes time, energy and planning to engage with our children and grandchildren, but it is well worth the memories and opportunities to share life lessons.

Today, my adult children know that they can always turn to me for positivity and support. They cherish memories of laughter and problem-solving. Our home might not have been perfect, but when challenges arose, they learned that we faced them together, consistently moving forward. Consistency, both in attitudes and actions, played a vital role in building the stability and trust that define our family.

Commitment to Consistency isn't just about being there; It's about being a rock-solid presence that others can always count on. Moving on to the next aspect of the CARE Strategy, let's explore Attractive Attention.

Coach Rob's Notes: "Diving into the CARE Strategy, the first pillar, Commitment to Consistency, emphasizes the importance of prioritizing people, managing reactions, and tracking commitments. This approach is time tested, not just in professional settings but also in personal settings, like social media and family life. By fostering a consistent presence, whether through daily accountability calls in a business context or engaging with family in meaningful activities, this principle cultivates reliability and trust. As we progress through the CARE Strategy, the focus on Attractive Attention next promises to further enrich our understanding of building and nurturing relationships. Remember successful people just do the basics better."

Attractive Attention: The Magnetic Force

While Commitment to Consistency focuses on reliability, Attractive Attention emphasizes being fully present. It challenges us to put down our phones and genuinely engage with those around us, whether in face-to-face interactions or through the realm of social media.

Steps to living Attractive Attention

- **Learn to Maintain Eye Contact:** Do you listen with your eyes and ears? It is important to give your full attention to the person speaking to you both in conversations online and offline.

- **Practice Hands-Free Interaction:** Keep your hands free from distractions during conversations to remain fully present.

- **Excel in Active Listening:** Listen carefully to individuals and repeat back what you've heard to ensure understanding and clarity.

I'll be the first to admit, I'm inherently an obsessive person. My natural focus and determination are strengths, but they can also be weaknesses. My husband quickly learned that when he enters my office to talk to me, he needs to capture my attention, or his words fall on deaf ears. My eyes must lock onto him, or I won't truly hear what he's saying. Being project-oriented, it was often a challenge for me to shift my focus away from work when my children were young. To overcome this, I learned to compartmentalize my tasks and finish my work during work hours, allowing me to be fully present with my kids without distractions. I discovered that paying attention was the key to nurturing our relationship.

Here's a real-life example that highlights the significance of Attractive Attention in our relationships. My husband is a deliberate communicator. He enjoys sharing jokes and stories at a leisurely pace. Even after forty years of marriage, it still requires considerable patience on my part to allow him the time to finish his conversations or questions before I respond. Paying attention has always been a personal challenge for me as I tend to get absorbed in my own thoughts and the direction I'm headed.

Over time, I've learned to prioritize my husband's words by watching him closely when he speaks, taking a deep breath before responding to provide him the necessary time to finish his statements, and repeating back what he said to ensure that I'm truly hearing and understanding his perspective. These deliberate steps have not only improved our communication but have also deepened our connection over the years. They underscore the essence of 'Attractive Attention'—being fully present and engaged in the conversations that matter most.

I've also found that the same principle applies to social media. When I pay attention to others, I attract them to me. People want to feel valued and that they matter. Building connections online is just as much about paying attention, showing genuine interest, and making friends as it is in the offline world. People are fundamentally the same, whether we interact with them in person or online.

Children will teach you that you must listen and take the time to focus; Otherwise, you might miss important signs of their thoughts and actions. Repeating back what I heard and clarifying their wishes has become second nature. It takes practice to truly listen to questions or comments before my mouth jumps to an answer. But in the end, the results are worth the effort. When you pay attention to others and prioritize their messages first, you attract more people and build a stronger community around you.

Attractive Attention is not just about listening; it's about making the other person feel seen and valued, a cornerstone of the CARE Strategy. In contrast to the previous pillar, Realistic Responsibility deals with accountability in a different way.

Realistic Responsibility: The Backbone of Dependability

To recap, we've discussed Commitment to Consistency and Attractive Attention. Now, let's delve into Realistic Responsibility. Realistic Responsibility calls us to take ownership of our actions, leaving no room for excuses or justifications. It's about acknowledging our stumbles, making amends, and being responsible for our commitments, both in the face-to-face world and on social media. Now, think about your own life. How do you manage your responsibilities, and what strategies do you use to stay realistic and accountable?

Steps to Living with Realistic Responsibility

- **Strive to Evaluate Realistically:** Do you regularly assess your ability to meet goals, and align expectations with the time and resources available? It is vital to understand what I can and cannot do.

- **Set Clear Expectations:** When apologizing, do I express my feelings honestly, do I focus on my actions rather than excuses, and have I established realistic priorities?

In life, we wear many hats—spouses, parents, grandparents, friends, and professionals. Each role brings its own set of demands, and the juggling act can often feel overwhelming.

As a mother and an executive, I came to a profound realization: I couldn't control time. We all have the same 24 hours in a day. What I could control, however, was how I managed the demands within that time frame. I adopted a systematic approach, relying on checklists and a love for processes. I broke down my life into manageable steps, taking it one day at a time. My year-long calendar held the big picture: Birthdays, projected vacation days, holidays, and school breaks. The monthly calendar added more detail, including activities and significant events. Then came the weekly calendar, where I delved into specific times for events. Finally, the daily calendar spelled out the nitty-gritty details for each project and commitment. Each night, I reviewed the next day's tasks, ensuring I was prepared.

In today's digital age, I've extended this organization to include a social media calendar. It outlines what posts I need to make on each platform and the type of content I'll share. It even factors in how many engagements I'll aim for each day. This deliberate planning not only keeps me on track but also helps me manage my time on social media effectively. It is easy to get carried away on social media and scroll through for hours instead of minutes. Setting a timer to track my time is beneficial.

I have also learned to take responsibility for the results on social media. Instead of blaming the algorithm for a lack of engagement, I take responsibility. I ask myself, "Have I been engaging with others?" The results are tied directly to my own engagement with others. Do I want results, then who am I engaging with to get results? If I want engagement, the question is, "Am I engaging?" The answer is simple. If I want reactions and comments, then I must be reacting and commenting!

Two valuable lessons became apparent to me along the way. First, understanding my responsibilities and being realistic about when I could fulfill them was essential. Overbooking and trying to be in two places at once were recipes for stress and chaos. Second, most stress stems from setting unrealistic expectations. Scheduling back-to-back appointments with no breaks or expecting to make school pickups within fifteen minutes of a meeting were simply unrealistic. Realistic Responsibility emerged as a vital principle for me, allowing me to maintain peace and stability in my daily life.

Realistic Responsibility is not just about meeting expectations; It's about setting them wisely and owning our journey, a crucial aspect of the CARE Strategy. So far, we've explored three pillars of the CARE Strategy: Commitment to Consistency, Attractive Attention, and Realistic Responsibility.

Engaging with Excellence: Elevating Connections with Sincere Support

As we've seen in the previous section, Realistic Responsibility plays a crucial role in managing life's demands. Now, let's see how it relates to the fourth pillar, Engaging with Excellence.

Engaging with Excellence extends an invitation to uplift others, to be a reliable and encouraging presence, and to contribute value through our social media connections. Whether it's through offering encouragement, entertainment, education, or empowerment, engaging with excellence has the power to transform ordinary interactions into extraordinary connections. Think of a time when someone's support made a difference in your life. How can you replicate that impact in your interactions with others?

Steps to Engaging with Excellence

- **Cultivate Gratitude**: Reflect daily on reasons to be thankful for others and how they enrich your life.

- **Celebrate Strengths**: Acknowledge and celebrate the positive attributes and strengths of those around you.

- **Share in Victories**: Actively listen to others accomplishments and join in their celebration.

- **Embrace Positivity**: Maintain a positive outlook, focus on solutions, and inspire hope in interactions.

Over time, I honed my communication skills, both in everyday life and online interactions. My social media mentor imparted a crucial concept that I've carried with me: Engage with others by sharing content that either educates, entertains, encourages, or empowers them. If I couldn't engage with excellence in mind, I refrained from sharing a post or starting a conversation. This principle has been instrumental in building my communication skills and fostering meaningful connections.

As my children have grown older, I've found that I have less advice to give them. I've learned to wait for them to ask for my opinion and to share what they need to hear rather than what I want to say. Their best interests aren't always the same as my opinions. As a grandparent, it can be challenging to resist the urge to lecture my adult children on parenting my grandchildren.

However, I've come to realize that they love their children just as much as I do, and they want what's best for them. I've learned to share stories instead of opinions, to believe in them, and to encourage them in their parenting journey.

Engaging with Excellence is a timeless principle that continues to guide me today as a parent, grandparent, wife, and friend. It's a skill set that I practice daily. Engaging with Excellence is not just a practice but a lifestyle, embodying the core values of the CARE Strategy in every interaction. Now that we've explored the four pillars individually, it's time to understand how they come together to form the complete CARE Strategy.

Nurturing Stability Through CARE

With a solid understanding of each pillar, we're ready to conclude our journey through the CARE Strategy. Life, with all its demands, calls us to a simple yet profound answer: Care about others' needs first. Putting the CARE Strategy into practice may not be easy. It will require a daily commitment to learn these skills, but the results will pay off tenfold.

Steps to Embracing the CARE Strategy:

- **Practice Self-Compassion:** Recognize that personal growth takes time. Reflect on your progress weekly, acknowledging both growth and areas for improvement.

- **Prioritize Honestly:** List your daily tasks and relationships in order of importance, focusing on the top priorities each day.

- **Choose a Focus Area:** Start by concentrating on one specific area or relationship where the CARE Strategy can be applied.

- **Build Habits Gradually:** Develop positive habits step by step, focusing on consistency for long-term change.

Throughout our exploration of the CARE Strategy, we've uncovered the transformative power of Commitment to Consistency, Attractive Attention, Realistic Responsibility, and Engaging with Excellence. This strategy isn't just about improving how we interact with others;

It's about enriching our lives with connections that are rooted in understanding, respect, and genuine care.

As we wrap up our exploration of the CARE Strategy, consider how these principles can enhance your relationships and interactions. As Jordan Peterson reminds us, we all have untapped potential. Embracing the CARE Strategy is a step towards realizing that potential in our relationships.

"You are more than you are today.
You are more than you think you can be."

- Jordan Peterson

Coach Rob's Notes: "Dora shares insights into living with Realistic Responsibility, focusing on evaluating abilities, setting clear expectations, and managing life's multiple roles effectively. Her journey, from a social media novice to a seasoned professional, underscores the importance of commitment and realistic goal-setting in fostering genuine online and offline connections.

Dora's strategic use of calendars for planning and her disciplined approach to social media engagement highlight her methodical method to life's challenges. She emphasizes taking responsibility for outcomes rather than blaming external factors, encouraging proactive engagement for desired results.

Her personal stories, from adjusting her parenting approach to engaging with her children and grandchildren's interests, reflect a deep understanding of meaningful interactions. Dora's experiences remind us of the power of realistic assessment and the impact of positivity and consistency in relationship building."

"Always build the people, and the people will build your business."

– Author Unknown

DR. ANASTACIA LEWIS

- Network marketing professional since December 2019.

- Achieved five-figure earnings in the first two months; Surpassed six-figure earnings within the first year.

- Leads a global team of nearly 200,000 individuals.

- Recognized as a Circle of Champions leader.

- Holds a doctorate in business and leadership.

I am Dr. Anastacia Lewis, a proud native of the Bahamas. With fourteen years of experience in the networking space, I find joy in connecting with people as my background is banking and insurance. Leadership is my niche, and I am dedicated to making a positive impact in this realm. I have served my company for the entire fourteen years and have decided to share winning strategies for the masses.

My advice for any person stepping into this space is simply this: Sit with the winners, the conversation is different.

I'm going to give you twelve key pointers for winning, so get a pen and paper and buckle your seat belt we're going for a ride all the way to the top!

Point 1 Mindset Matters

Make up your mind to win from day one. Winners understand that the conversation they have with themselves first is the catalyst to the journey of entrepreneurship. It's not just about positive thinking; It's about cultivating a mindset that welcomes challenges as opportunities for growth. Instead of viewing obstacles as roadblocks, winners see them as stepping stones to success. This mindset shift sets the tone for resilience, perseverance, and a proactive approach to problem-solving. It's about rewiring our minds totally to focus on possibilities rather than limitations. Winners constantly feed their minds. Buy network marketing books and attend leadership conferences so that your mind is right to be able to overcome any hurdle. This mental fortitude will become the driving force behind your positive actions influencing how you approach prospects. Success in network marketing starts not just with what you do, but with the conversations you have with yourself. Deal with you first then seek out a key leader to learn from and let's get this journey started. You must listen to winners and not whiners. Winners navigate the course of action and steer you through the obstacles so you get the results you want. Being open, coachable and of course a good attitude gets you to the top. There's nothing new under the sun. Someone has set the bar high. Now you go ahead and duplicate.

Point 2 Focus on Value

What do I mean by this?
Winners focus on value and approach network marketing to building relationships and providing genuine value to customers and team members. Unlike traditional methods focused solely on product

promotion, this approach prioritizes the creation of meaningful connections and delivering solutions that align with customers' needs. By establishing trust and rapport, network marketers can foster long-term loyalty and repeat business. In a value-centric model, the emphasis shifts from aggressive sales pitches to understanding and addressing the concerns of potential customers. This approach involves educating individuals about the benefits of products or services in a transparent manner, empowering them to make informed decisions. By positioning the product as a solution rather than a mere commodity, network marketers build credibility and authenticity. Furthermore, a value-centric approach extends to team building within the network marketing structure. You are a leader so you must prioritize mentoring, training, and supporting your team members to contribute to a positive and collaborative environment. This not only enhances the success of individual distributors but also strengthens the overall network. In essence, the value-centric approach transforms network marketing into a relationship-driven business. The value is in building people. Build the people and the people will build your business. Focus on the main thing. The solution is there and your commitment to serve. Keep the main thing the main thing.

Point 3 Learning is Continuous

When you show up you go up. If they don't appear they will disappear. In the dynamic landscape of direct selling, staying abreast of industry trends, marketing strategies, and product knowledge is paramount. Embracing a mindset of lifelong learning positions network marketers to adapt to changing market dynamics and evolving consumer preferences. Your job is to attend industry conferences, engage in webinars, travel with your company and read relevant literature to broaden your understanding of the field. Acquiring new skills, such as effective communication and digital marketing techniques, enables you to connect with a diverse audience. Moreover, staying informed about the products or services you promote enhances your credibility and empowers you to address customer queries with confidence. Remember, the network marketing landscape is dynamic, and those who invest in continuous learning not only stay competitive but also discover innovative ways to propel their businesses forward. Embrace education as a strategic tool, and you'll find that the journey of learning becomes a catalyst for sustained growth and professional fulfillment in the realm of network marketing. It takes real confidence and faith not only to stay abreast but some things we must also unlearn to relearn. Keep an open mind, things change quickly. You remain in that frame of mind and stick with positive people who force you to level up and focus on your personal brand and competence. It's not good enough just to be nice but functional globally. The work is yours and people who have achieved any level of success help you. They put the information in a book. Keep reading!

Coach Rob's Notes: "Dr. Anastacia Lewis showcases the essence of success in network marketing through mindset, value, and learning. She emphasizes starting with a winner's mindset, seeing challenges as steps to growth. Focusing on providing value over sales, she advises building genuine connections. Lastly, she highlights continuous learning as key to adapting and thriving in the ever-evolving industry. Her approach underscores the importance of resilience, authentic relationships, and lifelong education as pillars for sustained success. Lastly, she walks the walk with a team organization of over 200,000 members! She knows what she is doing."

Point 4 Create Authentic Relationships

Authentic relationships lie at the heart of successful network marketing business. Be yourself. People can tell when you are being fake. In this industry, building trust is not just a strategy; It's a fundamental necessity. Authenticity involves genuine connections, where network marketers prioritize understanding the unique needs and aspirations of their clients and team members. It's about more than transactions – it's about creating value and fostering a sense of teamwork and reciprocity. I help you and you help me. Authenticity resonates with people, as it transcends the typical sales pitch. Do not manipulate people to join you in business and spend excessive amounts of money just to help you get to the top, it backfires. When you approach interactions with sincerity, they build a foundation of trust that forms the basis of long-lasting relationships that goes beyond business and the industry. This approach not only leads to customer loyalty but also fuels the growth of a supportive network. Leaders who authentically support and mentor their teams create an environment where individuals feel valued and empowered. As a network marketer, embracing authenticity means being transparent about products or services, acknowledging limitations, and celebrating successes. Ultimately, the authenticity embedded in these relationships serves as a powerful catalyst, driving not only business success but also personal fulfillment and a positive reputation within the network marketing community. In a world saturated with marketing messages, authentic relationships stand out.

Point 5 Create Clear Goals

Setting clear goals is a foundational pillar for success in network marketing. Write down your goals every single month. If you can see it you can be it. Here's the thing: You must define both short-term and long-term objectives to create a structured and measurable path forward. Clarity in your goals allows you to articulate specific targets for sales, team growth, and personal development. Break down larger objectives into manageable tasks, making them more achievable and less overwhelming. This approach not only enhances focus but also fosters a sense of accomplishment as each milestone is reached. In the dynamic world of network marketing, setting clear goals enables adaptability. As you monitor your progress, you can adjust strategies, refine your approach, and pivot when necessary. Goals serve as motivation, driving you to push beyond comfort zones and capitalize on opportunities. Share your goals with your team to huddle. Make sure you initiate an intense sense of purpose and unity, aligning everyone toward a common vision. Regularly reassess and update your goals to reflect changing market conditions and personal growth otherwise you lose market share and credibility. This process ensures that your network marketing business remains alive, fresh and responsive. Ultimately, clear goals provide a framework for success, serving as a catalyst for continuous improvement, sustained motivation, and your team will realize and duplicate. You cannot want your team to do what you do not do. Intentionally write it down.

Point 6 Keep it Moving Don't Stop

Consistent action!!!!! Events, events, events!!! Winners understand that it's not the sporadic bursts of effort but the steady, relentless commitment to tasks that yield significant results. In the world of network marketing, where building relationships and trust takes time, the conversation shifts from occasional sprints to a marathon of consistent and intentional actions. This means daily engagement, whether it's reaching out to prospects, creating valuable content, or refining one's skills. Consistency builds momentum, and consistency makes you heavy and a credibility adds to elevating your brand which creates a ripple effect that fosters growth. When you consistently show up, your audience begins to recognize your commitment and reliability. Out of sight out of mind!! It's about setting routines and habits that align with your goals. So my advice is to get an accountability partner who will hold your feet to the fire to force you to level up in activity. Winners in network marketing understand that success is not an overnight phenomenon nor a lottery, but a culmination of persistent, disciplined efforts. People know when you are serious about your business. In the relentless pursuit of success, it's not the intensity of action but the consistency that transforms aspirations into tangible achievements. Believe it or not when you start and stop you push yourself back six months to a year and it takes time to get your momentum back. Sooooo keep it moving, don't stop!!!!!

Point 7 Sometimes You Have to Shift Adaptability

What is adaptability? Having an open mind to understand that things change and sometimes you have to shift it or you will get left behind. Winners in this field understand that the conversation revolves around being flexible, agile, and responsive to change. In an industry where trends shift, algorithms evolve, and consumer behaviors transform, adaptability becomes a strategic advantage. The ability to pivot, adjust strategies, and embrace emerging opportunities is what sets apart those who thrive. Be around team members who are constantly working so you hear when things shift. Stay connected to your company. Winners engage in a continuous conversation with the ever-changing market, acknowledging that what worked yesterday may not be effective tomorrow. They eagerly adopt new technologies, stay abreast of industry shifts, and evolve with the demands of the audience. This adaptability extends beyond external factors to personal growth. Embracing change is not just a survival strategy but a catalyst for innovation and long-term success. Ignoring industry changes and market changes is like hammering nails in your coffin and you to be buried. The conversation we all need to have with ourselves and our teams is one of resilience, curiosity, and a commitment to staying ahead of the curve. In a realm where adaptability is synonymous with staying relevant and ahead of the game. Winners not only navigate change but thrive in it, So we must have an open mind and keep our ears to the ground to gather the relevant information using each shift as a springboard for continued success in the ever-evolving world of network marketing.

Point 8 Leaders Show Up

Leadership presence is the heartbeat of success in network marketing. You want to lead a team you cannot be absent. Winners understand that the conversation they project, both verbally and non-verbally, shapes the confidence and trust of their team. If people don't respect your leadership they simply don't listen to you. It goes beyond titles; it's about embodying qualities that inspire and motivate. A strong leadership presence involves clarity in communication, transparency in decision-making, and a genuine commitment to the well-being and growth of the team. Again I say find a leader who you admire and learn so everyone feels heard, valued, and empowered. Leaders with a commanding presence lead by example, demonstrating the work ethic, integrity, and resilience they expect from their team. You cannot expect your team to do what you are not willing to do as accountability goes both ways up and down. This authenticity resonates within the network, establishing a foundation of trust and loyalty. The ability to navigate challenges with grace and to celebrate successes with humility is woven into the leadership conversation. It's about setting a tone that encourages innovation, continuous learning, and a shared vision. In network marketing, where relationships are pivotal, a leader's presence becomes the catalyst for unity, motivation, and the realization of collective goals. Leadership presence is not just about being in charge; it's about making a positive, lasting impact on the individuals who make up the network, creating an environment where everyone can thrive and succeed together.

Coach Rob's Notes: "Leadership presence, as highlighted, is crucial in network marketing. It's defined not by titles but by actions and attitudes that inspire trust and motivation. A leader must be visible, communicative, and genuinely committed to the team's growth. Emulating admired leaders,

embodying work ethic, and fostering an environment of transparency and accountability are key. This approach builds a solid foundation of trust and loyalty, essential for navigating challenges and celebrating successes. Leadership is about impacting lives positively and creating a thriving community."

Point 9 Effective Communication

Effective communication serves as the lifeblood of success in network marketing. Winners recognize that the conversation they engage in, shapes the perception of their brand and the strength of their connections. In this dynamic field, where building relationships is paramount, effective communication goes beyond words; it involves active listening and understanding the needs of your team and customers. Clarity is the cornerstone – whether explaining the benefits of a product or outlining the vision for the team. They tailor their communication style to match the preferences of their audience, ensuring a genuine connection. Moreover, winners leverage various channels, from social media platforms to personalized messages, recognizing that diverse communication strategies reach a broader audience. What I've come to realize is the cultural differences in communication as this is a global business so you must really foster great relationships so that you are not offending your leaders in different countries. Timeliness are also crucial; In a fast-paced industry, responding promptly and maintaining open lines of communication builds trust. The conversation revolves around building bridges, not just making transactions. Effective communication in network marketing is a two-way street, fostering engagement and collaboration. By mastering the art of articulation and listening, winners create an environment where ideas flow freely, relationships flourish, and the network becomes a community bound by shared goals and effective communication which reveals what went wrong and what is going right. The real deal is keep talking til you figure everything out.

Point 10 You Need a Coach/Mentorship

Mentorship is a huge deal for success in network marketing. This is your support and training ground for success. Winners understand that the conversation goes beyond personal achievements; it involves a commitment to both seeking guidance and providing support. Embracing a mentorship mentality means acknowledging that there is always room for growth and that learning from those who have navigated the path before can be transformative. Winners actively seek mentorship, valuing the insights and experiences of seasoned professionals. Simultaneously, they embrace the responsibility of being mentors themselves, fostering an environment where knowledge is shared, and growth is nurtured. The Law of Recognition speaks to acknowledging whose voice you should be listening to. The conversation within a mentor is one of continuous learning, constructive feedback, and a shared commitment to each other's success. It's about more than just transactions; It's about building meaningful relationships within the network. Sometimes it extends beyond formal arrangements and becomes a culture where collaboration thrives, and success is a collective achievement. Winners understand that the strength of the network lies in its interconnected support system, where individuals uplift each By embracing mentorship not only to accelerate their personal growth. Mentorship sometimes is one of the hardest things to do especially for professionals coming from their specific fields. They have experienced success already and they feel this industry is the same but sadly it's not.

Point 11 Accept the Challenges

Embracing challenges is a defining characteristic of winners in network marketing. Like any other business there will be challenges. I do not know of any person in business who does not encounter some type of challenge or drama. The conversation they have with adversity is not one of avoidance but of opportunity. Challenges are seen as stepping stones, not stumbling blocks. Winners understand that each hurdle presents a chance to learn, innovate, and refine their approach. Rather than being deterred by setbacks, they welcome them as catalysts for growth. The conversation revolves around resilience, acknowledging that the path to success in network marketing is not a straight line. Instead, it's a journey filled with twists and turns, requiring adaptability and a positive mindset. Winners don't fear challenges but they see them as indicators of progress. When faced with obstacles, their dialogue is focused on solutions and strategic adjustments. This approach not only propels personal development but also inspires confidence within their network. Words by the late Dr. Myles Munroe, one of my mentors, "Problems are an opportunity for wealth." By embracing challenges openly, winners cultivate a culture where everyone understands that overcoming difficulties is an integral part of the journey. The conversation shifts from complaining about problems to collectively finding solutions. In network marketing, challenges are not roadblocks but opportunities to shine. Winners use adversity as a tool for self-discovery and a catalyst for strengthening the bonds within the network. In the face of challenges, the dialogue is not one of defeat but of determination, resilience, and an unwavering commitment to achieving success.

Coach Rob's Notes: "Embracing challenges as opportunities for growth is crucial in network marketing, a principle I've discussed in The Game of Conquering. Every obstacle presents a chance to learn, innovate, and strengthen your resolve, mirroring the journey of any successful business person. Dr. Myles Munroe's wisdom, 'Problems are an opportunity for wealth,' underscores this mindset. It's about shifting the conversation from avoidance to proactive problem-solving, fostering a team culture where challenges are met with resilience and

creativity. This approach not only propels individual development but also solidifies trust and unity within the team, proving that facing adversity head-on is a testament to progress and a key driver of success."

Point 12 Celebrate Success & Go Global

One of my favorite topics is going global in network marketing. I'm excited because I have built a global team. A transformative step that requires a strategic conversation. Winners understand that expanding beyond borders means tapping into diverse markets and adapting to varying cultures. The conversation revolves around making money from anywhere around the world while appreciating the uniqueness of each market. The conversation about success is not just about personal achievements but about the collective triumph of the entire team spanning continents. How do we go global? It happens through technology, social media platforms and also organically. Every country has someone from another country who has settled.

Conversations and conversations events break the ice and foster building relationships and then partnerships. Advertise your business. You'll be shocked as to who is watching you . Your team members also allow you to go global conversation becomes a symphony of diverse voices harmonizing towards a common goal, creating a network that thrives on global collaboration and celebrates the success of each member as a victory for the entire global community. The real deal in network marketing is a global team.

I have so many more points to share as this is an ongoing learning process. All in all, winners help you to focus. So sit with them, have lunch, have dinner and in all that you do have fun in your business as you continue to build your empire!!!!!!

Love you all,
I'll see you at the top (and at the bank).

"If you continue to compete with others, you become bitter. If you continue to compete with yourself, you become better."

– *Anonymous*

ERIKA DALE

- Only had $226 in her bank account when she started network marketing.

- Today, team does $1.2 million a year in sales volume.

- Runs multiple online businesses with her husband Jesse as well as real estate investments and a cigar lounge.

- Erika's intentions are to help people step into the gifts God gave them and pursue their passions.

Back in 2015, I was working fifty hours a week to make ends meet. At the time, I couldn't figure out how to start a network marketing business. I didn't have that kind of time to sit in homes and go to meetings. That time was focused on going to work. One night, I decided I wanted to learn more about social media and how to maximize it in order to turn it into a side hustle. When I started, I thought, "This is a no brainer! It just makes so much sense." I didn't realize how many people were out there on social media. Over the past four years, I've been able to enroll over 630 people into my business through social media alone.

In my opinion, most people think social media will make it easier to succeed in this industry, but that's not always the case. Yes, you can build faster, get in front of more people, and receive more followers or likes but at the end of the day the basics stay the same. You have to build a relationship with your audience based on friendship while being a professional at the same time.

Coach Rob's Notes: "I've found that those who are busy tend to be more successful in network marketing than those who aren't. Busy people know how to utilize their valuable time. Put another way, urgency is synonymous with wealth. With Erika, she's laser focused on income-producing activities at the highest level. Go to www.sperrybonus.com to download our top eight income producing activities. These will open up your eyes. Also, make sure to read about Erika's ways to maximize the use of social media."

Don't be a Vanilla

I teach people to not be vanilla. What I mean is if everyone agrees with you (on social media), you're probably not being authentic or transparent with your content. That you're not saying who you really are. This will only push people away. Other times you may seem controversial to others with your posts. These are some obstacles you'll face when creating teams in your network. Don't be unexciting!

In one case, I had a couple people tell me they unfollowed me while another wrote how negative I was on my Facebook wall. I felt dumbfounded but got over it in a couple seconds. This business isn't for everyone, people are entitled to say what they want. No hard feelings. Not everyone is going to like you, and that's ok. Always be confident and know you're not always the right mentor for everyone. Aside from some of these challenges, keep expanding, put yourself out there, and create more value for your prospects.

When I was working in the gym, my reach was limited. Only 300 to 600 people a month were available to talk too. It was mostly the same people working out, and I realized it wasn't a good place for me to expand my network. The audience was too small. On the contrary, Facebook alone has 2.2 billion users. Imagine how many people you could reach there! That's a staggering number of users. When I rebranded online in East Asia, I connected with a customer in Taiwan. That customer sprouted more affiliates, and now I have a huge market in Taiwan connected to one of my Facebook groups. One of the ways I make a good impression with a prospect is by maximizing their value. I create rapport and become someone they know. When you search me on social media, you'll quickly find out how transparent I am.

Coach Rob's Notes: "People will judge you for being too fat or too skinny. People will judge you for being too poor or too rich. The mother of all fears is the fear of judgement. Get over it! As Erika pointed out, get comfortable with yourself. Be confident!"

Pick It, and Stick to It

Do yourself a favor, pick one platform and become the expert in it before you start dabbling in another. If you can't master one, then find another. I'm consistent at posting at least once a day on Facebook. Facebook is my business card and tells my customers I'm always open for business. Be consistent on your platform of choice and unlock the door for others to access your online business.

For the most part, Facebook encourages you to go live and host watch parties. Sometimes you'll get that notification. On my team, we host many watch parties and teach our members how to set up their own. You can show anyone the instructions manual as long as it's available on your forum. Your members may not be confident using it yet, but they can learn how to share it with their audience. Decide what works for you. Keep in mind, every system you put in place is another system you want others to learn. If you haven't mastered the platform, then don't take on anymore until you get the first one right. In other words, you don't want analysis paralysis. Find that one platform you feel confident with.

Principally speaking, some people enter my network marketing group with only five Facebook friends. They probably aren't going to be a social influencer their first year and that's fine! Over time they will reach that point. There's no timetable for success as long as your members put in the quality work to understand your social media platforms.

Consistently Follow Up

One of the crafts I teach my team is the "play team technique." For instance, if you see a team member's post, go like it or make a comment. The more likes and comments you make, the more visibility it's going to expose to your Facebook friends and groups. Keep in mind, Facebook allows you to see who can see your likes and comments by adjusting the necessary filters in the privacy settings. Adjust accordingly. To add on, algorithms and social media are always changing. Try not to allow yourself to get bogged down by that. These main platforms make sure their sites and apps are easy to use. The basics are still the same. Keep on posting, create videos, and connect with people on messenger. Without effort, there's no gain!

As several hours go by on my post, I wonder how many crickets are in the room. I wonder if the internet is broken! If you post and aren't

getting many likes or comments, you can message your friends or followers to check it out. Ask them to like or make a comment.
Do your best to get your content out there in front of your network. The more engaging you are with your audience (friends, followers, group pages, etc.), the more they'll respond back. A Facebook broadcast will usually do the trick. Be a student in the art of social media. New applications are introduced every hour on the app store. Do your due diligence and stay up to date on new software that may aid you in your business network.

On occasion, I've had several people in my downline ask what active promotions are currently available on my posts. These are great questions to ask if you're doing really well in your business. It comes to show those who ask questions are the ones who have better results in comparison to those who don't ask questions. In other words, do your best to share with your groups often. If you don't, you'll slowly lose your members as they'll feel less motivated to work with you. I try to post more than once a day, but not more than thrice a day. Be flexible. Spread your posts at different times of the day. If I post all at once, then I wait 3 to 4 hours before the next post. Basically, if you post at 7:00 am and then an hour later at 8:00 am, people won't see that 7:00 am post due to Facebook's algorithms. The idea is people aren't going to your timeline and scrolling. You need to let that post marinate to let your audience have a chance to like it and comment. The same Facebook algorithms apply to everyone using this platform. Make sure to post throughout the day.

I strongly recommend having a Facebook group page for your team and one for your prospects. At times, I'll combine my customers and prospects together because it's a great way to upscale and integrate your team. Eventually all prospects become members, but I believe a prospect group is necessary. It doesn't have to be fancy and you don't have to pay someone, you just have to start. Ask everyone to post on the group. Give them ideas to post about. Assign an administrator every two weeks and make that administrator pick a new one for the next two weeks when their time is up. This is a good way for everyone to feel integrated as a leader and will give them an opportunity to introduce new team members. Other times, I'll put my customers and prospects together since my prospects sell to customers. Open the channel for your prospects.

Life Happens Outside of Social Media

By and large, you have to work on improving the quality of your content if you're not seeing the results you want. Besides learning on social media, reading books, listening to podcasts, going to company events, being part of the community, do the masterminds or get a coach. When you're learning, you are able to yield back the knowledge to your affiliates.

What I love about Facebook the most is you can bond quickly. People get to know you by what you write and post. If you aren't writing stories yet, then start! Quite often I see posts written with "my." This context will say, "like my product" or "like my post." There's no connection with people here and my husband struggled with this. He would get frustrated since he would go live, make a post, and not get any traction. I asked him if he was reaching out to his audience afterward, liking and commenting on their posts. He said no. He wasn't scrolling on his feed to see what his friends were posting. The point is, you have to be intentional online and in person. Eventually I taught my husband to like and make comments on his audience's news feed five minutes before he made a post or went live. By doing this, he was able to attract more people to his post or livestream, rather than one person to none. He saw the difference and thanked me by making my favorite food dish!

To get to the topic at hand, if you want to receive engagement, you must first be engaging. You wouldn't go out with your friends for lunch to only talk about yourself all afternoon. The best approach is to ask them questions, be interested and contribute. This identical theory bears similarity to any other platform. Don't be the person that's all about you! Be interested. Live a life where you connect with others by sharing the same space, talking about each other, sharing your plans and showing your integrity.

Coach Rob's Notes: "Erika and her insights remind me why I initially didn't have success on social media. For five years I didn't post one thing that would help my business. I was fearful for doing it the wrong way. Finally, I woke up and committed to posting every day. When I did this, everything changed. Sure, I had some pretty awful Facebook posts at first. When the date came, they popped up as annual Facebook memory posts. Meanwhile, as I started to post daily, the quality of my posts improved. They became more authentic, engaging to watch, and my audience noticed my niche! To be honest, I only fabricate my posts in five categories. If there was something that didn't fall into one of those categories, then I wouldn't post it. The objective is about consistency. At first, you won't be great, but if you stay committed to posting daily on one platform, your audience will start to notice."

"Don't be bitter, get better."

– Author Unknown

JOHN MELTON

- Top 50 earner in the entire profession.

- Top 3 in his company.

- Member of the Network Marketing Hall of Fame.

- Team stats for the last 6 years: $295+ million in sales and 780,000+ new customers.

- Team stats for the last 12 months: 73,030 new customers & 4,035 new social marketers, 68 of whom are personal recruits.

7 Tips For Massive Duplication: Help Your Network Marketing Team Have The Biggest Month Ever

How would you like to create your biggest month ever? No more excuses! You're ready! Yes, you're ready for a breakthrough, ready to rank up, and ready to have the success you deserve!

I know what it feels like to go from having almost no results to absolutely crushing it. I've been there. The journey can be challenging, but it is immensely rewarding. That's why I'm here to share with you my seven best tips for massive duplication that will help you and your Network Marketing team create their biggest month ever! Let's dive right in!

Tip #1: Set a Team Goal

The first step to achieving massive duplication is setting a team goal. Determine how much revenue you want to generate as a team. Understand the goals of the individuals within your organization.

For instance, if you have a team of 10 people and each has a goal to do $5,000 in volume, that's $50,000 for the month! Your goal should be to help as many people in your team rank up. Identify those who are serious and committed, and work with them. Break down the goal per sale per day.

Let's say your target is $100,000 this month. That's $25,000 a week. Break it down per person. If you have 100 people committed to doing $1,000 in personal sales, that's $100,000 in your organization.

When you set clear, specific, and achievable goals, you provide a roadmap for your team. It's like giving them a GPS for success. They know exactly where they're headed and what they need to do to get there. That clarity is a game-changer.

Coach Rob's Notes: "Setting a clear team goal creates a unified vision. It's essential to break down these goals into manageable daily actions, providing a roadmap for success. Accountability and celebration of small wins are crucial to maintaining motivation and momentum within the team."

PRO Tip: Have an accountability chat with your team. Hold each other accountable and give each other shoutouts! Accountability is key to maintaining momentum and achieving your goals. When everyone knows they're being watched and cheered on, it adds a layer of motivation and commitment.

Remember, a team goal isn't just about the numbers. It's about creating a shared vision and a sense of unity. When your team works towards a common goal, it builds camaraderie and a sense of belonging. It's not just about individual success; it's about collective achievement.

Tip #2: No Excuses, No Distractions

How badly do you want this? Having fun with your business is great, but how serious are you about getting your best month ever? If you're in a place where you don't want to be and you're sick and tired of being sick and tired, the solution is simple: No excuses and no distractions!

Many Network Marketers suffer from "excuse-itis." They constantly question their abilities and make excuses for why they aren't where they want to be. The truth is, it's a mental game. Get out of your own way and say, "Enough is enough. I'm not making any more excuses for why I'm not working my business or why I'm not where I want to be."

When you cut the excuses, you will start to see success. Focus on your goals, eliminate distractions, and commit to your business wholeheartedly. It's about discipline and determination. Think about it—every time you make an excuse, you're essentially giving yourself permission to fail. But when you decide that excuses are no longer an option, you open the door to success.

Excuses are comfort zones. They're the little lies we tell ourselves to stay comfortable. But success lies outside of that comfort zone. It's about pushing yourself to do the things that others aren't willing to do.

It's about working late nights and early mornings. It's about making sacrifices and staying focused, even when distractions are tempting.

One of my favorite sayings is, "Suck it up, buttercup!" It's a tough-love approach, but it's necessary. You have to be brutally honest with yourself and your team. If you're not where you want to be, it's time to change that. No more excuses. No more distractions. Just pure, unadulterated focus.

Tip #3: Be Fearless

To achieve massive duplication, you need to be fearless. Talk to everybody, make bold statements, and get comfortable with being uncomfortable. When talking to people, say something like, "I'm serious about this business. I'm committed, and I'm looking for people who are looking for me. In other words, I'm looking for people who want to change their lives."

Yes, it can be uncomfortable. It can be difficult to have those tough conversations, especially when someone is questioning things. Simply say, "I get it. You're skeptical. I was skeptical too, but I want to help you. If you're serious and coachable and follow the system, I will work with you and help you succeed in this business. Let's work on it together!"

Even some people already on your team can be difficult. But if you want to be successful, you have to be fearless. Boldly approach prospects and teammates alike with confidence and clarity.

Being fearless isn't just about talking to people. It's about taking risks and stepping outside of your comfort zone. It's about trying new strategies, even if they might fail. It's about putting yourself out there, even if you might get rejected. Fear is natural, but it's how you handle that fear that makes the difference.

One of the best ways to overcome fear is to focus on your "why." Why are you doing this? What's driving you? When you have a strong enough "why," the fear becomes insignificant. Your desire to succeed outweighs your fear of failure.

Coach Rob's Notes: "Being fearless means stepping out of your comfort zone daily. It's about leading by example and showing your team that taking risks and embracing discomfort leads to growth. Your courage will inspire others to push their boundaries and strive for success."

Fearless leaders inspire fearless teams. When your team sees you stepping up and taking risks, they'll be more likely to do the same. Lead by example. Show them that it's okay to be bold, to make mistakes, and to keep pushing forward.

Tip #4: Be a Content-Creating, Curiosity-Marketing, Prospecting Freak of Nature

Let's repeat that because it's crucial. Be a content-creating, curiosity-marketing, prospecting freak of nature! Use Instagram and Facebook Stories, go Live, create TikToks and Reels, engage with different Facebook groups, friend up people every day, and prospect, prospect, prospect!

Talk to 3, 5, 10, 15 people a day (not a week) about your products or business. Whether you lead with the product or the business is up to you. But you need to do it every single day.

Put out content daily. Wondering what to talk about? Share tips, success stories, and insights related to your business. Consistency in content creation will make you more visible and build your brand.

PRO Tip: Do both marketing and prospecting simultaneously. This will create a strong brand and attract people to you. The more you engage with your audience, the more comfortable you will become with creating videos, putting yourself out there, and sharing your story.

In today's digital age, content is king. It's how you reach people, build relationships, and establish yourself as an authority. But it's not just about creating any content—it's about creating valuable, engaging content that sparks curiosity and drives action.

Curiosity marketing is about creating content that makes people want to learn more. It's about sharing just enough information to pique their interest and leave them wanting more. It's about creating a sense of mystery and excitement around your products or business.

Prospecting, on the other hand, is about being proactive. It's about reaching out to people and starting conversations. It's about building relationships and identifying potential customers or team members. The key is to balance both—create engaging content to attract people and actively prospect to build your network.

Tip #5: Help and Recognize Your People Like it's Your Job

Remember what it's like to be new. Reaching out to your first few people, getting your first few customers, doing your first curiosity post, or your first Facebook Live video can be daunting.

Recognize your people for their wins, no matter how small they might be. Your main job should be to help them rank up — help them get their first recruit, help them get their first customer. It all starts with recognizing the little things. Celebrate every victory and encourage your team members to keep pushing forward.

Recognition is a powerful motivator. When people feel appreciated and valued, they're more likely to stay committed and motivated.

It's about creating a positive and supportive environment where everyone feels like they're part of something bigger.

Think about it—how did you feel when you achieved your first milestone? Probably pretty amazing, right? Now imagine how your team members feel when they achieve theirs. Celebrate those moments. Make a big deal out of them. It shows your team that you care about their success and that you're there to support them every step of the way.

Helping your team doesn't just mean recognizing their achievements. It also means providing the resources and support they need to succeed. This could be training, tools, or just a listening ear. Be there for your team. Guide them, mentor them, and help them grow.

Tip #6: Stay Positive

Drama in teams is inevitable, but staying positive is essential. What you pay attention to will grow. Focus on positivity and cutting out excuses, and you will start to see better results.

As the saying goes, save the drama for your mama! While you can't completely ignore it, try to keep it positive when you get involved. Keep everyone levelheaded and focused on their goals. Positive reinforcement and a supportive environment are key to maintaining high morale and motivation within your team.

Negativity is like a virus. It spreads quickly and can infect your entire team. That's why it's crucial to create a positive culture within your team. When challenges arise, address them with a solution-oriented mindset. Focus on what you can control and how you can improve.

One of my favorite quotes is, "What you focus on, expands." If you focus on the positive, you'll attract more positivity. If you focus on the negative, you'll attract more negativity. It's that simple. So choose wisely. Celebrate the wins, learn from the challenges, and keep moving forward.

Creating a positive environment also means encouraging open communication. Let your team know that it's okay to share their struggles and challenges. Provide support and guidance, and encourage them to keep pushing forward. When people feel supported and understood, they're more likely to stay positive and committed.

Tip #7: Keep Pushing

Keep going and keep pushing! Don't slow down. Keep talking to people, keep using the ATM system[1], keep doing Group Chats, and putting out content. Stay positive and focused. Recognize all the efforts of those who are working hard.

You don't have to convince anyone to commit and build their business. Some people on your team might not be as motivated. Even if you benefit from their success, you can't want it more for them than they want it for themselves. Keep pushing till the very end.

W.I.T. Baby! Whatever It Takes!

Persistence is key in Network Marketing. It's not about having a perfect plan or always knowing the right answer. It's about showing up daily, doing the work, and pushing through the challenges. It's about staying committed to your goals, even when things get tough.

---

1   ATM stands for Add, Tag, Message. You Add people to a Private Group, Tag them in a video you want them to watch (that explains the products/business/ etc.) and then Message them to see what they liked best.

Remember, success doesn't happen overnight. It's the result of consistent effort and determination. Keep pushing, keep learning, and keep growing. The journey might be tough, but the rewards are worth it.

The one question I want to leave you with is this: how bad do you want it? Are you:

- Talking to new people every single day?

- Putting your upline in Group Chats?

- Fearlessly asking your leads prospecting questions?

If someone is doing all these things, I know they are working! This is why I love the ATM system! I can see my teammates tagging people in the Groups. This allows you to really lock arms with the runners, get fired up, and get them where they need to be!

If you help enough people have success, you can truly have the biggest month of your Network Marketing career!

Coach Rob's Notes: "Persistence and consistency are key. Engage with your team, celebrate their efforts, and provide continuous support. By fostering a culture of relentless pursuit and mutual encouragement, you pave the way for sustained growth and monumental achievements."

Are you fired up to get your biggest month yet? Go crush it!

"You can have it all,
but you can't do it all,
and you can't do it alone."

— Rhonda Britten

JULIA THORNHILL

- A former marketing director and Navy SEAL, parents of 2 littles, Brandon and Julia are pioneering a faith-based team spanning over 20 countries, fostering 100+ organic 6-figure earners and distributing nearly $100 million in commissions to their organization.

- They are celebrated for hosting a multitude of transformational events for their team, including marriage retreats, women's empowerment gatherings, masterminds, exotic retreats and leadership bootcamps.

- Achieving their company's highest leadership retention, they are renowned for revolutionary systems and a bold, vibrant culture of parents who love to travel the world and experience life with their kids.

- Raised nearly $1 million for humanitarian causes, combating human trafficking, and aiding hungry families worldwide.

Hi friends! My name is Julia Thornhill (call me, Jules!) and I'm here to share a piece of my heart with you. My husband Brandon and I have been instrumental in nurturing over 100 six-figure earners and multiple seven-figure achievers in the realm of network marketing. We have held the highest retention in leadership for years in multiple countries and have helped families earn almost $100 million online in the product space. 98% of those people did not have any experience. Yes, we built everything from scratch. No handouts, no big business given, nothing. Just raw creation from the ground up.

Imagine crafting a business that not only weathers the storms of recessions, pandemics, and world crises but emerges stronger and more resilient. In a world full of mundane, underwhelming Zoom calls and rah rah old school hype, the need for more intention could be just the solution.

Here's the deal – you can learn the skills, teach the tactics, and sprinkle in mindset wisdom, but it's the infusion of intention that keeps the growth flowing. This isn't just about business; it's about the people. It's about painting a canvas of possibilities, reigniting dreams, and holding space for others to dream again. It's about believing in their potential even before they catch a glimpse of it. Trust me, once you believe, you can lead. In a world full of mundane, underwhelming zoom calls and rah rah old school hype, the need for more intention could be just the solution.

In our world, it's not about transactions; It's about transformations. Which brings me to what I believe is a bit unique behind the scenes and can help ANY organization increase retention after being a part of the best masterminds in our industry.

This includes:
Events
Committees
Unified Mission
AUTOMATIONS

All with MASSIVE intention behind them, Jesus with a dash of
Tony Robbins.

My background is in marketing and my husband was a Navy SEAL for
twelve years. He grew up in a trailer park, I grew up on food stamps. We
lacked mentorship in all areas of our life. To date, we have invested about
$500k in personal development and over the last eight years we found
a good balance between each other. I, Julia, am the events, visionary,
systems-obsessed leader and my husband is the hard coach; the hammer
with a huge heart and the one that says the things someone may not want
to hear but needs to hear to become the best version of themselves.

We've been asked countless times, "What are you doing differently?"
So, let me spill the beans on what's uniquely brewing behind the
scenes, infused with a lot of Jesus and a dash of Tony Robbins.

On almost every event or team call, our goal (outside of just helping
others making money or getting results on products) is to help people
in seven specific areas of their life. These are not mine, they are based
on Tony Robbins *7 Areas of Constant Growth for an Extraordinary Life.*

So let's break it down and how this can apply to your business:

- Health and Vitality

- Mind and Meaning

- Love and Relationships

- Productivity and Performance

- Career and Business

- Wealth and Lifestyle

- Leadership and Impact

I believe that people can make 6-figures a month in this industry but if they're not growing, if they don't feel valued, if they're a part of something bigger than themselves or if they're not walking away from your calls, events, and interaction they won't last.

Coach Rob's Notes: "Julia Thornhill, whom I know well and have immense respect for, exemplifies what it means to be a solid leader in network marketing. Her approach sets a benchmark for creating not just a successful business, but a thriving community."

Julia and her husband Brandon's journey from humble beginnings to nurturing over 100 six-figure earners is an unreal example of their commitment to personal development and leadership.

Their focus on transforming lives across the 7 Areas of Constant Growth, shows the importance of development in achieving extraordinary success. Their strategies, emphasizing events, committees, and a unified mission, all driven by massive intention, is a powerful blueprint for any organization looking to improve retention and foster a culture of continuous growth. Julia's narrative is a reminder that the heart of network marketing lies in the people and the potential transformations within them, urging leaders to believe in their team's potential, even before they see it in themselves.

So what I want to do first is to break down a few ways we help our team improve in those seven areas of their life in regards to events for each category. Let's dive in, shall we?

1. **Health and Vitality:** We're in the mental wellness space, so that probably won't align with your world too so for those of you in different niches, consider incorporating health initiatives like drinking a gallon of water a day or the seventy five hard

challenge for your teams. You could even start your daily calls with an attitude of gratitude.

2. **Mind and Meaning**: Lots of mindset training for this one Monday through Friday for ten minutes before our daily calls every day. We also make sure our monthly regional calls always have a session on this. Let's be honest, this business is 90% mindset, 10% skill set. You can have the best tools, apps, gadgets and training but if their mindset isn't right and they are going into everything you're training on with the wrong intention then it's a waste of time. It's like a ship without a compass.

3. **Love and Relationships**: During our launch process people are assigned mentorship, accountability partners and through our events they build the most amazing friendships. Our marriage retreats, leadership bootcamps and family experiences heavily create this more than any zoom can. Proximity is power. Experiences are everything. This is one of my favorite parts about this business, it's the conversations I've had with my team around a campfire in Jackson hole or on a yacht in Dubai about our kids (preferably all our kids are there too). This is what I always pictured, building a community you can trust your own kids around. Trips and experiences around the world and memories created. I'll dive more into events shortly.

4. **Productivity and Performance**: We like to do time management training (especially with kids). Lots of different tools, training on A.I. and accountability challenges. I believe that you also need to build the business with the things that bring you joy, first. So rather than put all the things you need to do to move the needle forward, instead, put all the things that bring you joy. For example, write down in your calendar

this week the things that make you happy. For example: Skiing, playing with your kids, date night, the gym, self care, etc. After those are booked, then put in what needs to get done for your business. This will allow you to avoid resentment, burnout or push things behind that are important to your overall mental wellness and happiness. The happier you are the better you'll perform!

5. **Career and Business**: We are all relevant here! We all run businesses, however, there are more effective ways to do that. Running a business does not mean burn out. Running a business means being efficient with your time with the little time you have, especially if you are building it around a traditional job. In this life factor, this is where your mission and vision can come in that I'll get to. This is where people believing they are a part of something bigger than themselves can contribute. This is where getting your teams involved in all the moving pieces it takes to run can aid in them feeling valued and growing. This is also where your events can come in to play to help improve their overall life in so many ways.

6. **Wealth and Lifestyle**: For wealth, we do yearly wealth summits and tax education for this one. The goal is not to teach someone how to make ten thousand dollars a month and spend it all, the goal is to create more FREEDOM. If someone earned a company car, it doesn't mean they go get the car, you know? For lifestyle, we do paid-for trips to Dubai and spoil our six-figure earners or anyone who's earned over $100k with red bottoms or custom suits. You can get creative here. It could even be heavily promoting your company trips. Don't overthink it. I also believe you should heavily involve your kids if you're a parent. They should know the ranks and when you hit every milestone. Make it their promotion too. Every month or two go do something fun! It can be as simple as going to get ice

cream and camping or as extravagant as flying to Europe (if it's in your budget). We like to go on trips every ninety days. Not team trips (those are fun too) but trips that WE plan as a family. This allows them to be involved in the growth and also be involved in the milestones. If you have older kids, write down what they would want to do and throw it in a hat - the more you can get them involved, the better !

7. **Leadership and Impact/Contribution**: Outside of our leadership retreats and bootcamps, this is where our committees come into play so keep reading.

Now that we've tackled the seven areas intentionally, let's dive right in and start with EVENTS.

To date, We've hosted a plethora, hundreds – from grand conventions that cost over $100,000 to intimate team gatherings. The size doesn't matter; it's the impact that echoes. Here's the playbook from largest to smallest in regards to attendance:

1. **Team Only Event at our Company Convention**: We always have our own breakout and launch new tools, incentives, do recognition, etc.

2. **Our Yearly Team Event aka Wealth Summit and Branding Workshop**: It's like a convention just for your team. There have been times where our team event was bigger than convention! It's been titled wealth summit for several years and then tacking on a sub category has been new.

3. **Leadership Bootcamp**: I love the breakdown, breakthrough and build up technique. Think adult summer camp but ten times better.

4. **Customer Appreciation:** We have executed several events, from wellness workshops to renting out entire water parks - we want our customers to feel a part of our mission and to feel appreciated. The water park was a blast since our community involved tons of parents so it was a great day to hang out with all of our families. We set up stations so our customers could experience products they may never have had and we got our partners all involved to play an important role in executing such a unique experience!

5. **Team Qualifier Retreat:** These are usually at exotic locations for just our team built around corporate incentives. Try not to work against the company, only complement it. For example, if the company has an incentive with a points system they are tracking, work in similar qualifications and when they hit a bigger milestone, you offer a trip!

6. **Marriage Retreats:** I believe the family unit is more important than ever and since the majority of our top leaders are couples, we've run several to strengthen their marriages. Our most recent was in Park City and was over valentines weekend.

7. **Masterminds:** This is for our CEO council and some of our head of committees. We dive into everything from systems, events and challenges to what's mapped out that year. I've brought in catering, massage therapists and photographers for brand shoots.

8. **Core Family Events:** This is an event for all our top earners and their kids. I.e. We rented a chalet in deer valley, went skiing and catered the weekend. This is more of a fun event to just create memories. There isn't much business talk here even though it's hard to not because we love what we do so much, but this is more an event to get to know our team's families and their kids more. The overall goal is to just create memories together.

9. **Charity Events:** I believe that if you're blessed, be a blessing.
    Our team has raised over half a million dollars to fight human
    trafficking and feed families. Some ideas you can take on that
    we've also done is rally behind a charity your leaders or team
    votes on. We have also done local charity events and seasonal
    events around the holidays to give back, from toy and clothes
    drives to volunteering at local charities. You can get different
    countries and cities in your team to have a friendly competition
    on most donations raised. Tis the season to always give back!

10. **Virtual Events:** From Women's workshops to Mental Wellness
    Masterclasses, we pack a ton of value into them and are great
    for guests. This is usually a soft introduction to our products,
    programs or community. The events are usually two to three
    hours long online or in person. We may even bring in outside
    trainers but the goal is to give value to our community. Some
    topics we've trained on are time management, wellness for busy
    moms, goal setting, etc.

11. **Weekly Team Calls:** These are always pretty similar:
    Announcements, recognition, mindset, skill set and call to
    action. Thirty to forty-five minutes max. I think it's important
    to get the new people up there sharing their story. A
    testimonial (not a "trainamonial") one to two minutes max
    sharing their story, not a ten minute preaching session. These
    can get carried away so coach accordingly!

12. **Daily Team Trainings Monday through Friday:** The basics,
    mindset, skillset, social media, etc. This also trains the trainers!
    Most of my six-figure earners do these calls and rotate. I
    encourage them to bring up their new people on the calls as
    well so they are feeling seen and valued.

Phew! I hope that gives you a few ideas to incorporate.

Just know that these events we run are not always every year. We have always done our big team event and then we chose another event like a leadership bootcamp but the rest all determined the season and what the team needs and leaders want to execute.

Coach Rob's Notes: "Julia Thornhill's event-driven approach to network marketing is not just innovative; it's a comprehensive blueprint for achieving six figures and beyond. This strategy is centered around making an impact, fostering community, and enhancing the personal growth of team members. The span of events, from wealth summits to marriage retreats and charity events, showcases a deep commitment to not just business growth but personal and communal enrichment as well. Julia's focus on incorporating intention in every aspect, backed by her and Brandon's inspiring journey and investment in personal development, offers a model that's ripe for replication or adaptation according to your business's phase."

Whether you're directly implementing these strategies or envisioning them as part of your future growth, the essence lies in the transformation they promise—not just in business metrics but in personal lives and community well-being. This chapter offers invaluable insights into creating a culture that celebrates learning, achievement, and genuine connection, embodying what it truly means to lead with intention and purpose.

With that said, let's get straight into committees. This is one of my favorite ways to make your leaders feel valued and as if they have a voice and important role in the overall mission.

A committee is a collective of empowering individuals on your team, providing a voice, fostering a sense of purpose, and preventing burnout. It's a volunteer force, not a hired team, and certainly not a platform for mere complaints without solutions. This is a volunteer army, not a "you're hired" situation. It's also not the "complain with no solution" show. It's not the "I bring you the problems Jules and you you do it" show. It's the, "I'm in the trenches and have amazing ideas to enhance our mission" show.

Here are some tips:

1. It does not necessarily have to be a rank, although usually 50-100k sales a month is ideal.

2. Three to five people per committee. Too many cooks in the kitchen is exhausting.

3. Have them commit quarterly. This allows them to be replaced if they do not bring the value or show up at any given time.

4. Personally call them and invite them.

5. Have the committee vote on when to meet (once a week max, every two weeks is better).

6. Have a head of the committee member that runs it, you don't need to be micromanaging people. You didn't enroll to run an adult daycare center. You want to empower people with their God given gifts!

Here is how I currently run my organization top down:

CEO Council: The movers, the shakers, the innovators, the drivers, no more than three to five positions. Most of our six-figure earners are couples, so there will be more seasons, but these are my generals. These fluctuate every one to three years.

Communication Committee: They create all team challenges, documents, flyers, slide decks, boards, facebook groups, text chats and chats, etc. Usually working directly with my graphic designer.

Social Media Committee: You guessed it, social media. Tik tok and reels challenges, templates, ai prompts, etc.

Events Committee: From decor, to speaker flow to the whole vibe, they execute (I also usually bring in an event coordinator that works with the committee).

Customer Committee: this group manages the facebook groups, approves testimonials, goes live weekly, fosters giveaways and challenges and keeps things fun!

One-offs:

Gear committee: t-shirts, swag, etc.

International committees: (this is key when expanding globally). I believe that there are things in different markets that can only be seen by that country. Having a committee in place can help scale things faster and get systems in place. You just need to make sure the person running them is trustworthy and educated enough to work with your designer. You don't want to reinvent the wheel here, you want to polish the wheel and maybe add a new rim if you know what I mean. It's easy to complicate and harder to simplify.

So that's it with committees. Think of them as a way to not wear all the hats but allow others to wear them. I think one of the hardest parts in leadership is wanting everything done perfectly. What I've learned over the years is to be okay with things being done 80% right. It's better than being done 100% and being burnt out. Learn to delegate not demand and learn to let go and let God.

Lastly, let's talk about the MISSION and VISION. I believe that you can create, craft and cultivate ANY community you want.

The Bible says "without vision people perish". I believe it's the same for creating a community that lasts.

"Now let's talk about UNIFIED MISSION" With that said, here's who I hire on salary, hourly or monthly to work with the committees and keep me sane with two little girls under three:

- **Project Manager**: Overseas all operations and Virtual Assistant

- **Virtual Assistant**: Pulls reports, creates chats, monitors FB groups, organizes calls, attends committee meetings, etc.

- **Graphic Designer**: this person pulls content from the comms committee and creates everything from beautiful graphics, and team regional flyers to facebook cover photos & recognition templates, etc.

Throughout my career I've started different movements. I've been successful in all of them but one. When I say "successful", I define that as: Successfully gathering hundreds and thousands of people coming together on Zoom or at events for a common purpose and goal. I'm talking about bringing people together with actual integrity to change the world for good. Most of you are picking up what I'm putting down (you're my people). So you'll want to dial in your mission and vision.

Eight years ago my husband and I said we wanted to "create a community of faith-based couples we can trust our own children around". This was an internal vision I prayed on and it came true.

To date, my 3 year old has been on over 50 flights, 10 countries: fourteen states and most of those trips were with our top earners and their kids. They were either paid for by the company, our events or because we just love each other and our kids are all best friends from around the world. Subsequently, almost all 100+ six-figure earners we've created have been couples.

My point of mentioning that is we were clear about a year in on what the community we wanted to create looked like. In the beginning, it was a crazy, wild learning experience that stretched our minds to what was capable for our life.

Overtime, we got really clear on who we wanted to work with and experience life with around the world.

So let's take some time now to figure out what that is for you. However, I want you to think about for a minute if you were direct to the company (and maybe you are) but imagine there was no upline support, no calls in place, nothing. Imagine from scratch right now that you could create a beautiful community. What does that community look like? What are their common problems, beliefs, fears, desires and dreams?

Your mission statement is the heartbeat, clearly articulating what your organization does and who it serves, embodying the essence of 'We do [X] for [Y].'

Your vision statement is a glimpse into the future "Envisioning the ideal future state and expressing what your organization aspires to become, encapsulating the essence of 'We aspire to be [X] in [Y].' "

So take a moment and think about this.

My community today is very much bold in their faith. We take the faith over fear approach. Lead or be led. The "We trust our community, not the government" vibe, if you know what I mean. Homeschooling is skyrocketing for a reason and I'm so here for it.

With that said, I should mention that it has evolved over the last eight years and in my opinion, I think reinventing your team, just like your own personal brand, is a good thing.

So, for example, one of our mission statements has been this: *We are "Unmasking the truth about Mental Wellness and Financial Fulfillment"*.

Vision: To create a million healthy, wealthy, happy homes.

Boom. No fluff. No confusion. You know what you get. Most of our banners at our events have "FAITH. FAMILY. FREEDOM" on them because that's what WE believe that's how it should be - in that order.

Is everyone in our community obsessed with it? No. But the majority are, and that's okay if not everyone is. You can have sub-cultures in your team which I also believe is powerful.

Aim to empower your community over blowing up your own ego. It shouldn't be the YOU show. This is about the PEOPLE. It's about showing others what's possible.

Lastly, let's talk about AUTOMATIONS. This is where more time with your kids comes into play. This is where simplicity with your systems will help. This is what leaders love to come into I could write an entire book about our systems, but I'll dive in to what we're doing now that's working extremely well that could help with your onboarding and duplication :

1. **Launch & Onboarding**: We have an Automated Launch system for every new partner w/ automated text & email sequence with exactly what to post to generate leads for NWM & non NWM. Daily Reels organized by hooks & Posts with captions & specific reply methods per engagement. And short 3-5 minute Video Modules to get onboarded on your schedule & plugged into resources.

2. **Brand Creation**: On Day 10 of our Launch w/Leads System - we teach our team how to Dial in Your Niche/Storyand then provide them with a 30 Day Content Calendar with hundreds of examples. We use A.I. Brand/Target market Prompts to find your customers desires & pain points to create curated content and offer Dozens of Advanced Trainings & Courses each year + LIVE Branding Workshops.

3. **Content Creation for Lead capture**: We have a Funnel Quiz for Social Media that captures your leads with hundreds of pieces of content to share and capture. We offer Thousands of pieces of content categorized in an app for simple posting: brand, product, NWM Transition, Business, etc. We provide Faceless marketing videos, Project Broadcast & Advanced Automation Prompts with manychat. And we also offer new Courses each quarter: Advanced Automation, Time Management, Leadership, Wealth 101, etc.

If you've stayed with me on this journey, you're ready to wield the pen, script your story, and build a community that harmonizes with your soul, I bet you have what it takes. You have one of two things; that burning desire to change the world or the desire to be a part of something powerful.

Perhaps for the first time you're realizing that YOU get to choose. That YOU get to pick up the pen and write your own story. That YOU get to create ANY community you want, and I believe you can too. Just remember, lead with love, intention, integrity and purpose and sometimes you just need to let go and let God.

Xoxo,
Your friend,
Jules
Aka Julia Thornhill: wife, mother, fierce friend and God-fearing proud network marketer.

Coach Rob's Notes: "Julia Thornhill's story is a powerful example of leading with intention in network marketing. By centering her approach on faith, family, and freedom, she and her husband have cultivated a community that not only excels in business but also in personal growth and shared values. Their focus on creating meaningful events and nurturing specific areas of life is a strategic blueprint for anyone looking to build a cohesive and motivated team.

For effective leadership, clearly define what your community stands for and weave these principles into all your actions and events. This method builds more than just a business; It fosters a network where every member can flourish. True leadership is about empowering your team and providing a platform for shared victories. Keep your vision and integrity at the forefront of your efforts, and watch as your community strengthens and expands."

"If you don't sow, you don't reap."

– Jim Rohn

LANCE CONRAD

- Top recruiter out of a million distributors.

- 16 years industry experience.

- Built business in 40 plus countries.

- Helped 400+ people earn a six figure income over the last 3.5 years.

- Took a company from 0 to $100M in 13 months.

Everybody Hates Network Marketing and It's Not Your Fault

When I first got into network marketing, I was 33. A friend of mine called me up and said, "Hey, let's go do skincare." He was 27. Every 27 and 33-year-old wanted to sell facials, but he was brave enough and bold enough to make it big enough that I was interested. It ended up becoming a partnership, and it changed my life and sent me on a journey around the world where I've trained over a million people around the world. That was Rob Sperry, who had the guts to call me. That was extremely brave. I owned my own business. I had ten employees, and he was gutsy enough to call me. I was the first person he called. So, I want to talk about that. I jumped into that company, and there's nothing wrong with skincare. I love skincare. It's consumable, so people use it every month. Skincare companies are great companies, and now that I'm getting older here, I could use more skincare in my life. But at that point in time, it wasn't like I woke up that morning and said, "I'm going to go do facials."

Little did I know, this leap into skincare was just the beginning of an unexpected adventure. I jumped in, and the first four people I called said yes. I said, "I'm doing this. You're doing this. Give me your credit card. Say yes, we're doing it." It was a $1,600 buy-in for that deal. I thought I was off to the races. I hit the first rank. I made like $900 in twelve hours. I'm like, "Oh my gosh, sell my business. Quit everything. I'm a full-time networker. This is going to be great." So then I called those four people up and said, "Okay, so who are your four people? When are we going to talk to your four people?" I got crickets. "Oh yeah, well, I'm busy. I'm at work. Call me later." So that was like at eight in the morning. So at nine thirty, I'd call them again. "Okay, who are we calling? Where are you for? When's our meetings?" Crickets, noon, eight. Crickets by three. I'm like, "Shawnee, you're my sister. I know you speak English and I speak Spanish. Oh, sorry, you got to go," and she'd hang up on me. Pretty soon those four people didn't want to talk to me anymore. Okay, so what happened? I recruited followers, I recruited customers. I recruited people into my business that didn't have that same level of commitment in my business as I did. I wanted to make millions of dollars with it. That's why I joined. Of course, that's why everybody else would join. Those people were not the right people to go build monster teams with. So I started recruiting customers. I started recruiting followers. I started to build a team, and then I had a training where, look, if you could bring five fantastic people into your business, five influential people into your business, five people that really are going to treat it like a business, it will make you millions of dollars. My fave five.

Alright? I was recruiting the wrong people. I was talking to the wrong people. I was trying to find customers. I was trying to find followers. What I needed was leaders. This is the leadership business. If you find customers and you find followers and you are building a business that you are going to have to babysit for the rest of your life, but if you get true leadership into your business, you've created true leverage and it will take on a life of its own.

Realizing the need for a strategic pivot, I decided to take a more targeted approach. So, I went home and made a list. Now, I had some pretty good people on that list, and I thought, "Alright." I was a recruiter, a headhunter. Four of my best friends were recruiters or headhunters. They'd been good at recruiting people. "Man, I'll just put this team together." By the way, I'd made all of them a lot of money. They were really good friends. They'd made me money in some cases, but we'd been partners for a lot of years, and I figured, "Man, I'll get them in my business. I'll launch my business, and I'll be done. I can retire, right? It's just that easy, right?"

So, I called Casey, Mark, Chad, and Nadine. Now, these are good friends, not okay friends, business partners, longtime friends, who I made a lot of money for. All four of them said no. No, they didn't just say no. They said, "Heck no." No, it was worse than that. I couldn't even get them to come to meet with me, not to a meeting. But if it was a meeting about networking, they didn't want to come. One of them laughed at me. One of them said, "Really? Is it that hard for you right now? Do you need a loan?" Like they were worried about me, but all four of them just flat out shut me down.

What are you going to do, right? There's my wishlist, there's my chicken list, there's the guys that I was going to build and the lady that I was going to build my future around, but they're not the most influential people that I know. So, I put on my list this guy named John. Now, John had just become famous in our state. He had just sold his company for hundreds of millions of dollars. We're talking about a 30-year-old, somebody in his mid-thirties that's worth over a hundred million dollars, like liquid cash money done. He's got every car in the garage you could possibly want. I actually told him when I went to his garage that he had all the posters that I had growing up, and he's like, "I know nothing about cars. That's what I did. I went out and bought all the posters," so Lambo, Ferrari, Porsche, all that.

So I went and pitched John why he should join my business with me and how it would change people's lives and how it would be the most fulfilling thing he ever did. Guess what? He shut me down. Okay, so what did I learn? Well, I learned that after I had those conversations, talking to anybody else became so easy. I had just got shut down majorly by my biggest chicken list, my biggest people. But talking to an average person at this point, I was like, "Oh, okay. What's the worst they can say?" It was no, and I'm still friends with all those people. So the world didn't end. It didn't stop turning, and now it made it easier to talk to other people. The other thing that did is it changed my expectations of who I was looking for and who to work with. So I was recruiting, building, going until I found this guy named Robert. Robert was young and he was just crazy enough to talk to anyone. He put me on with a guy through somebody he knew and somebody they knew. He put me on with a lady named Diane. Diane was a really successful realtor. All of a sudden, I found a leader, a partner, somebody I could run with, and I hit a rank and it was about 25,000 to 30,000 of volume with that lady in her first month, which is about what I did in my first month, which made about a $10,000 check.

Coach Rob's Notes: "Lance Conrad's path in network marketing emphasizes the power of daring to act and the strategic choice of recruits. Jumping into the industry at 33, after a call from me, he began his network marketing journey, quickly learning the importance of selecting leaders rather than finding anyone interested.

I learned more from Lance than any other leader in network marketing. I lacked confidence and boldness but borrowed from him until I had my own. As a close friend who introduced him to network marketing, I've observed Lance's development into a significant figure in the network marketing profession. Most network marketers go for what we call the low hanging fruit. Those who will for sure say yes. Lance shows the opposite is not just possible but is another way for many to have success."

Suddenly, we had a story, and I had someone who was moving as fast as I was, treating it as a business just like me, and my business began to change. We attracted other leaders. She brought in a lady named Tiffany. Tiffany went and hit about a 25,000 to 30,000 volume rank, which made her about seven to eight thousand dollars. Then the next month, we did it with someone else. Then the next, all of a sudden, we were attracting leader after leader, influencer after influencer because we were setting that expectation. When we talked to these people, it was a different kind of conversation. It wasn't about this little networking thing; it was big. We were talking about market share, about cities, states, countries. We discussed how to grow a business starting from a local market, then expanding into another local or nearby market, and then growing to other states. From there, we were taken across the country, and suddenly we were talking about distribution, market channels, partnerships, strategic partnerships. You'll notice the language I'm using is not typical network marketing language. I'm talking to influential people. These were not professional network marketers. So, I wasn't using network marketing speak. I wasn't talking CV, PV, TV—don't do TV; it just crushes your business, right? I was talking about strategic partnerships, about market shares, about cities, states, countries. If you could really do well in your city, you could make hundreds, if not thousands, of dollars. If you could do well in your state, you could make thousands of dollars. If you could do well across the country, you could make tens of thousands of dollars a month. If you could do well internationally, you could make a hundred thousand dollars or more in monthly income. We were looking for strategic partners. You're probably thinking, "Oh, but I'm not you, and I can't talk like that, and I don't have that credibility." Knock it off! Stop making yourself the issue, right?

So here's the point. It's not about you. It's about your company. You're in a great company, or you wouldn't be there. It's about your product. What's your company's history? What's your company's total sales? What attracted you to that company? What's the product? What is the new product, the hot product, the sexy product? What's the product that people are getting excited about? So, you stop making it about yourself; make it about someone else. That way, if they reject it, they're not rejecting you; they're rejecting a company or a product. Make it about your upline, but don't say upline; say your strategic partner. So, you have an opportunity to put the right people in front of the right partnership, right? If you do that, see, now you are making it big. I always made network marketing really big. I said, "I need to meet with you today or tomorrow. Next week never comes, and next month, forget about it." They're going to have ten other excuses that come in the middle between now and next week. So, if you don't make it today and you don't make it tomorrow, just forget about it. It's never going to happen. If it's so big that it's going to be life-changing, if it's that kind of opportunity, you want them to make time in their schedule, not try to fit you in the cracks of their schedule. I've shown up on people's doorsteps at 10:30 at night that I barely knew or didn't know referrals to have a meeting because that's when they were available. I would tell them, "Look, I'm going to make millions of dollars with this business. I'm looking for partners that want to go to the top with me." You know what they'd tell me? "I believe you because you're here at my house at 10:30 at night." So, if you make it big, they'll treat it big. If you make it small, they'll treat it small. So here's the list. I'm going to give you some lists, some takeaways, a challenge, and I'm running out of time. I could just tell stories for hours.

I got better at bringing in influencers from there; I've brought in the right influencers and been able to build teams of 10,000 plus people. One of my last big blitzes, I did that in less than a month. We did $972,000 of volume with no pre-launch with one right influential person, but really, a leader is worth more than thousands of followers. I would trade whole teams of people to be able to partner up with the right people. If you change your mindset and your expectations, you're going to realize that leaders attract market share. They attract followers; they attract everything else that you want within your business, and finding the right leader is worth the chase because it will change your business and it will change your life.

So, who do you want in your business? You want people that are already influential, that already have circles of influence and have credibility within those circles of influence. So, write this down. You want anybody that's made six figures annually in any walk of life; put them on your wishlist. Fitness professionals, teachers, coaches, pastors, priests, professional MLMers that have made over $5,000 a month—these are the people I'd put on my list. I'd go make a list. Your fave five, the five people that you most want in your business. Write them down. This is your chicken list. Guess what? We're going to dust it off. Now, here's the great thing about it. There are two questions everybody asks themselves: Can I do it? Is it worth it? These people already know they can do it.

So, you've just got to show them that it's worth it. The timing's right, the product's right, the partnership's right. You've just got to show them part of it. The other thing about it, they don't get hit as often. If it's your chicken list, it's everybody else's chicken list. They're not getting hit up nearly as often as you might think, and they're going to look at it with more fresh eyes than you think. The next thing I would tell you, get other people involved, especially if you don't have a check, if you don't have a ranking. Then your goal is to sell the appointment. I need you to meet my friend who's made millions of dollars in this industry. I need you to meet this executive at this company that helps partner with me and helps us create market share. Because I believe you could do this in the seven-figure annual type income, which the top leaders in this company, that's what they make.

We're looking for strategic partners to open up the Western states, the Eastern states, to open up South America. You need to make it big. You need to make it bold. You need to be confident about it. Don't make it small. If you're going to bring on a partner to do a three-way call, I guarantee you that they're willing to do it for your chicken list, for your best people, just about anybody is willing to talk to them. If you've already addressed what your company is, what it sells, and that you've already made them the big kahuna, that they're the person you want to partner with, that they're the ones that have made millions of dollars. So, if you prep it so that by the time they do the three-way call, it's not a cold call.

I don't care who it is, anybody in your upline will do it, but don't put them on a cold call. You'll waste their time, you'll waste your credibility, and you'll never get a three-way call with that person again. So, sell the appointment, make it really big, make the pitch really short, and then sell the appointment. Don't make yourself the issue. Make your company the issue, the product the issue, the timing the issue, and the ability to work with the strategic partner. Make that the issue.

Here is the challenge: I want you to call five people on your chicken list over the next twenty four hours. You need to do it now. You need to get courage. You need to get brave, all with the goal of just getting them to look at the opportunity. That's your job, not to sell them, not to close them.

Make it big enough that they go see it. I'm working with somebody that's made X number of millions of dollars in this business, and you need to meet them. I believe you have more skills than even they do. If I partner you up, there's no telling what you could do. We've got the hottest product in the marketplace right now, and the timing's fantastic. If you meet this person and get trained by this person, there's no stopping you. See, you notice it wasn't about me. It wasn't about partnering with me; it was about the company, it was about the product, it was about the partnership. So, I'm going to give you a good, better, best challenge.

Good is to reach out to five people on your chicken list in the next twenty four hours. That's good because it took some bravery, and you might get shot down just like I did. All my first five people all shot me down, but it raised my expectations and made all my other calls easier.

Better would be to get in front of or get on a real pitch. Hey, I reach out to them, that's good. If I could really make a presentation and really make a pitch to them, that's better. I would keep it really short, three minutes or less with the call to action or get on the next webinar or get to the next meeting. But if you really make a presentation with a call to action to five of your influential people, just like pat yourself on the back, that's better.

Best is to do a three-way call or any type of three way validation with an upline mentor, or to do a face-to-face presentation, ideally with an upline mentor that could bring credibility, that could bring PACK to the punch, and that could help you close that deal.

This is what I can tell you. Five influential people in your business will make you millions of dollars. One good person can help you bring tens of thousands of people to your business. I would trade thousands of followers for one strategic partner that's going to treat this like a business, that has influence, credibility, and is going to run with it with full heart. It's really going to treat it like a business. So, is it worth it? A hundred percent. It's worth it. Will it grow your business so fast? Your head will spin. You'll just be trying to keep up with it. The worst that they can say is no. If you don't call them, they already said no. But if you do call them, it will give you courage to call other people. It will raise your expectations on who you're bringing to the business. You will start to attract other influencers, and they might not be as big and as credible as your first ones, but eventually, you'll attract people way better than they ever were. So do it. Do it now. Do it today, and watch your business explode. Thanks, guys. Make it a great day.

You're not just flipping through another chapter on network marketing; you're stepping into an arena where the timid fear to tread and where the bold reap rewards beyond their wildest dreams. Every giant leap begins with a small step. And in the world of network marketing, we all start from the same spot: Zero. But here's the thing— where you start doesn't determine where you'll end. It's the hustle, the grind, the relentless pursuit of excellence that carves your path from zero to hero. Guess what? If I can do it, so can you.

Coach Rob's Notes: "Lance Conrad's narrative illustrates the power of reaching beyond comfort zones. It's an example of the "go big or go home" attitude that defines many success stories in network marketing. The concept of contacting those on your "chicken list" embodies the boldness required in this profession. It's not just about making those new calls; it's about what those calls make of you—a more resilient, ambitious, and fearless entrepreneur.

Through Lance's eyes, we see a strategy unfold: Reaching out to influential individuals can exponentially accelerate your business growth. His "good, better, best" challenge lays down a practical roadmap to engaging these key players. It's a call to action for embracing rejection, leveraging mentorship, and harnessing the potential of strategic partnerships.

As someone who personally knows Lance and has witnessed his journey, I can attest to the efficacy of his approach. His courage to reach out, coupled with the strategic mindset of utilizing upline mentors for credibility, sets a blueprint for making significant strides in network marketing.

Remember, the journey to the top is paved with bold moves. Lance's advice isn't just about growth—it's about transformation. It's about how stepping out of your comfort zone and into the realm of possibility can lead to untold success. So, embrace his challenge, step up to the plate, and let your actions today ignite the fuse of your explosive growth tomorrow. The world of network marketing loves boldness, and as Lance shows, boldness coupled with strategic action is an unbeatable combination."

"The blessings are in the follow-up!!
And they flow both directions!"

– Rita L Goad, PhD

RITA L GOAD, PHD

- Rita was a 'hard no' for Network Marketing for many years... until a trusted friend invited her to take a closer look, and followed-up with her.

- Entered Network Marketing profession in 1994.

- Has enjoyed working with multiple companies, learning from each experience.

- Has been blessed to earn incentive trips & cruises to fun destinations such as the Bahamas, Puerto Vallarta, Cancun, Arizona, Utah, Dominican Republic, Cozumel, etc.

- Conference speaker.

- Author/ co-author.

- Built to elite level offline, before social media, and again online with social media.

- Married 45 years.

- The mom of 4, and a gramma.

- Gardening consultant, homeschooler, researcher, avid traveler, singer/song writer, entrepreneur to the core, leader, mentor, friend.

- Rita's passion is growing strong, healthy families and she especially loves helping moms build health and wealth.

The Blessings Are In the Follow-up

Coach Rob's Notes: "Rita is the master at following up. She practices what she teaches. Too many distributors don't have success because they won't master the boring necessary tasks to do so. I was approached by reps of eleven different network marketing companies before I joined my first one. Out of the previous eleven, there were three that I was ready to join, but the person who contacted me never followed-up. They lost out on a massive income simply because they didn't follow-up."

Network marketing and farm life have something in common: They both require a lot of hard work! I grew up on a farm and learned to have an entrepreneurial spirit from my dad. He loved being his own boss and living his dream life on the farm, and he was willing to work hard to make that happen.

When I started network marketing, like most people, I was intrigued by the business model, but I didn't know exactly what I was getting myself into. This is a real business that takes hard work. Unfortunately, many people aren't willing to see it that way, or to do what it takes to build significant income. They are hopeful that it won't actually require work.

Me too! Ha! I always thought it would be great to be paid to be a bum, but that isn't reality. That is not how success in anything happens.

I learned another important skill working alongside my dad on the farm: Follow-up! Follow-up is key to success! Farm work is never done. You never get to simply check a task off the list and move on. We were constantly following up on the farm. The animals all need follow-up, the chores need constant follow-up, the fields need follow-up... season after season... year after year.

Whether you are working on a farm or building a network marketing business, follow-up is vital. For decades in network marketing I've heard the phrase, "The fortune is in the follow-up." To me, this doesn't fully paint the vision, because that phrase focuses only on me. The complete picture of success goes beyond focusing on me. We benefit most by recognizing follow-up as the way we bless prospects' lives. I like to say, "The BLESSINGS are in the follow-up, and they flow both directions!" I often remind my team about this. When I don't follow up with my prospect, I keep them from having the blessings they could have with the product or the business.

Consistency is Key

Currently, experts say it takes an average of twenty-one touches or exposures for someone to get a "yes" to their offer in network marketing. That is a LOT of follow-up! You do have to be a source of information for your prospects in follow-up conversations, but it goes beyond this. Ask yourself, "Why would this person want to talk to me instead of going to Google or YouTube to get their questions answered?"

This doesn't mean that you have to talk to your prospects twenty-one times about the tool or product. Rather, it means multiple touches through personal conversation, which also will include tools and resource sharing. Consider all follow-up as relationship-building conversation. Show sincere interest in the person, and in what they are doing and going through in their life right now. Weave the blessings you have to offer into life conversations naturally and intentionally. Don't ignore the fact that you need to talk about the business. But, don't mention it every time. You want people to be happy to see you. Do stay in front of your prospect with your follow-up one way or another.

I have a couple of key phrases I use to help take the pressure off of the prospect and help me not feel pushy. If I haven't heard from someone in a couple days after sharing the product or business info, I say, "I don't want to push, but I also don't want to leave you hanging. Is there any additional information you'd like to have from me?"

If it seems the prospect is avoiding continuing the conversation, I like to say, "If this isn't a fit for you, no worries at all! Would it be cool with you if I keep you updated on how things are going?"

Getting people interested in this business takes time. It is rare that someone wants to jump right in. People are busy, and our business and/or product is never as important to the prospect as to you or me. You and I are the ones that have to make follow-up a priority.

Be focused on the activity of following up, and don't get hung up on the results. If you do the activity enough, the results will follow. Consistency matters, and follow-up is all about consistency. If you can stay consistent, it puts you FAR above the pack. Very few people will be consistent with their follow-up. Be one of the few!

Sometimes it takes months, even after the customer or prospect has said they want it. You have to be willing to focus on the activity and continue to commit to the process. Never think that following up gets to be checked off the list. Never stop the conversation!

Coach Rob's Notes: "Reread this sentence, because it is pure gold. "Sometimes it takes months, even after they have said they want it." You are playing the long game! This is a process. Some say yes right away. Some take a few weeks, and some take much longer. The follow-up process isn't done even if they say no. Huge tip here. If one says no, then ask that person this. "It sounds like right now isn't a great time for you. Are you ok if I keep you posted on everything?" This gives you permission to follow up later. Now don't misinterpret what I am saying. Don't pitch this person the next week. Instead set 2 reminders in your phone to reach out non-business related. One reminder in a few weeks and another reminder in a few months. No one likes the network marketer who approaches them every year about their products or business without any conversations in between. They perceive that network marketer as a TAKER. There is no set time when you should approach this person again as there are many variables. It could be four months later because you are just checking in. It could be sooner because you had a new product launch that you think would interest them from a customer or even business builder standpoint. The main point is be a good human being and remember that the follow-up never ends!"

Follow-Up Will Build Relationships

Follow-up is a relationship-building skill. There are several key relationships that you want to follow up with: Your community (local and social media), your prospects, your customers, and your team. It is all about making connections and staying in front of people. Think about how you can connect and follow-up with people in your local or social media community. Are you being a blessing and really supporting people in the community? Are you being intentional with your time in the community? People may not be in enough pain right now for the product or the opportunity to be a great fit. But, when they are, I want to be the one they think of for a solution and someone that is interested in helping them. This is the real reason for the follow-up. We want to be a blessing in people's lives! If I am not consistent in connections and follow-up, then they may think of someone else when it is the right time.

I love social media. I have built my current business almost exclusively through social media. In 2017, I had no clue how to do that. I just jumped in and began learning! You can do the same and start to utilize more of the tools you have available to follow up with your prospects and customers.

Messenger has made it so easy to connect to people without having their phone number. Using this, we can text, call, or send video and audio messages. It has been such a huge time saver. I remember homeschooling my kids by day and leaving my house at night to build my business the first time I did network marketing. I see social media as such a blessing because now I don't even have to leave my house as I build a business. It is such a joy knowing several moms on my team have been able to come home and build their business from home while being with their children! Be willing to step out of your comfort zone if necessary to learn the current tools and use them.

It can be scary or intimidating for some folks to learn something new. When I learned about social media, I watched other people and started listening to training about how to use it. But even when I jumped in, I really didn't know what I was doing. I just kept thinking that if they can do it, I can do it. Now, follow-up is more convenient and less time consuming than ever before!

Have a willingness to jump in and make 'mistakes'. This is literally the only way to learn and build new skills! You must be willing to fail in order to grow and succeed!

Social media is a huge blessing, but often people forget that you MUST follow up on social media. People misunderstand social media. It can be so helpful in building relationships, and the skills are basically the same as if you were sitting together in a coffee shop! Communicate regularly. Be a friend. Massively utilize written text, audio message, or video to stay in touch and be a good, thoughtful human.

Few people get positive uplifting things from anyone. I will send a quick message to people and tell them good morning, or tell them I am praying for them today. I simply send a quick positive message and they often send back a huge message telling me about what is going on with them. People are craving connection. I want to emphasize to people that social media is all about building relationships and being a blessing.

You also have to follow up with your team. This is non-negotiable. Reach out to your team. If you have a large team, reach out to maybe ten a day. Do it intentionally and purposefully, on a schedule.

This is a key skill of a leader. If you have one partner or one customer on your team, you are a leader. Start to follow up with the relationship and commit to continuing to follow up with them as your team grows.

Follow - Up With Your Own Training

One of the blessings I am most grateful for is the personal growth training I have experienced in network marketing. I don't know who I would be today without it, but I do know who I am because of it. Even if I hadn't made any money, the personal growth alone is worth the money and time I have spent. Personal growth takes truthful follow-up with yourself. You must hold yourself accountable. No one is going to check in with you to see if you are doing your own work.

You just have to do it. Take total responsibility for all of it. You have to listen to coaches and trainers, and then you have to do the work. It goes back to what I talked about earlier. You must be consistent. I can go train a whole group of people, but it isn't the training that is important. It is what the individual is willing to do with the training that matters. It matters how they follow up with themselves.

I would love for it to just all work for everyone. But, the reality is, you have to be willing to do the work yourself, for the long-haul. That is what is going to make anyone successful, including you. We can all do better. We all have room for growth.

This industry has so much potential for the long-term. We need to help paint the picture for people to start to see the business for what it actually is. People are looking for a short-term huge success. It can happen, but for most, it doesn't happen quickly. Start with no less than a 5-year plan and commitment. Be willing to be the example of hard work and dedication to your follow-up system and you will find success in the long-term.

Rob's Notes: That's leadership. Lead by example. Follow up. Don't be weak and give false hope. As a leader, emerging leader, or future leader, you must cast a vision that this is a real business. This is not a quick-fix overnight type of business. There are huge benefits to those that treat this like a real business and match their work ethic to their dreams.

*"Die with memories,
not with dreams."*

– Rob Sperry

TRACY RODGERS

- Started network marketing in 1988 and failed forward for 32 years.

- Got out of the industry for a few years and became a merchant marine.

- Went back to the industry in 2017 & helped launch a company and in the five years there built a team of 40,000.

- In 3 years was the first to promote to the top rank.

- 7 figure yearly earner.

- Started her own company in 2022.

Coach Rob's Notes: "What Tracy doesn't share with you is that she went from not making any money in network marketing to homeless to top earner. She went from homeless to a top earner within one year. She has one of the most powerful stories I have ever heard. I was able to watch her journey and see her massive progress. In the last two years, I have seen this woman speak LIVE in Mexico, Maui, Sundance, Utah, Canada, and Australia. This section is going to be all business and straight to the point. Learn how she recruits and closes!"

Sharing the Opportunity

This industry is perfect for anyone seeking a second stream of income, a six-figure salary, or the freedom of more time. Over the years, our industry has evolved with new technology, environmentally conscious products, and the rise of social media. Yet, one thing remains constant: The power of building relationships.

There's something truly inspiring about gathering with like-minded people, boosting each other's confidence, and creating a thriving business together.

In my thirty six years of Network Marketing, I've uncovered the key ingredients to reaching the top: Passion, Sales, Recruits, and Personal Development.

Before sharing the opportunity, let's talk about passion. When you share your product, do your eyes light up? Does your voice pick up speed and excitement? Do you wholeheartedly believe in your company's mission, its leaders, and the compensation plan? Do you feel the urge to tell everyone you meet about it? If so, you've already tapped into the most crucial element for success. Your passion for what your business has to offer will make sharing the opportunity natural, seamless, and inviting.

An Offer for Anyone

One amazing fact is that a side gig like Network Marketing can be for anyone! The possibilities are limitless, and you can take your business as far as YOU want. Our "whys" and goals are unique and constantly evolving, depending on our needs and the growth of our business. I've often heard people say, "I was going to just use these products myself, and before I knew it, I was making the extra money our family needed."

Recruiting 101 – this is where sharing the opportunity begins. I'm passionate about sharing this opportunity with everyone! It doesn't matter what they do with it; I can offer the opportunity to ten different people with ten different goals without feeling pushy or guilty because this isn't about me, it's about helping others. If I don't offer it when I get the chance, then I've ultimately made the decision for them, never giving them the chance to hear the possibilities. I am a rock-star recruiter because I am genuinely excited for people to have the opportunity to do what I do!

Being empowered to start a business and grow it has so many rewards. Team members have gained confidence, escaped abusive situations, supported their families when a spouse lost their job, relieved financial pressure, and discovered what is possible for them.

THIS is what sharing the opportunity is all about. It's not just about making money; it's about giving someone a chance to say yes to changing their own life. It is not my place to decide for them. If they say yes, then we can discover their vision together! This is why I love this industry so much. My goal is to change one life at a time and together we can all make the world a better place.

Coach Rob's Notes: "Don't prejudge anyone! Can you imagine someone prejudging Tracy? She hadn't had success in network marketing in thirty three years. She was homeless. She is a perfect example of why you should be willing to share your business/products with everyone."

The Fave Five

"If you build it, they will come." Recruiting becomes effortless once you establish genuine relationships. Many of us crave community and meaningful connections. When you engage with others as your authentic self and share your excitement about your product or opportunity, people naturally become curious about what you're doing.

My Fave Five method is simple, doable, and easily duplicable. Each month, you start fresh, and by the end of the year, you've connected with sixty people, shared a bit of life with them, and either welcomed them to your team or received referrals for potential team members or customers.

Let's get started! Each month, pick five people you think would be great at this business, who you'd love to work with, or who really need something like this in their lives. Focus on building a relationship with them. Throughout the month, send voice clips (people love hearing your voice), texts, and comments on their social media posts. Show genuine interest in them as individuals, building that crucial know, like, and trust factor. I keep a notebook to jot down what they're posting, their pain points, and any financial needs, giving me insights when I connect with them, so they know I'm listening and genuinely care.

When you see a post on Facebook where they are sharing a "proud moment" – a child graduating, a new puppy, a new car – comment on the post and take it to Messenger to expand on their excitement. This starts the relationship-building process, making them eager to engage in the conversation. You'll also feel good about building an authentic relationship, eliminating any sense of being salesy or spammy.

As the relationship builds, you can introduce the business by saying, "This may or may not be for you, but you may know someone who could use the extra money or would be great at this. I'd love to give you a little information so you can make an educated decision." Opening with "This may or may not be for you" lowers their defenses, gives them an easy out, and opens up the conversation.

Close the Deal Questions

Are you ready to transform your recruiting process? How many people do you have sitting on the fence right now? They're interested, they've asked questions, but they haven't signed up yet. To move forward, you need to uncover what's holding them back. I've discovered the power of one simple question:

"Let me ask you a question. You mentioned before that you're interested in joining our company. What is the one thing stopping you from getting started and making money next week?"

For example, if the top objection is "I don't have enough time," you could respond with, "If I could show you how to build this business with the time you normally spend on Facebook, would you be open to that?" Once you know what's holding them back, you can address it and help them move forward.

I know this sounds crazy, but it WORKS! This one question can help you overcome any objections they may have. Some people might feel uncomfortable asking it at first. You need to practice and find the words that fit your style when sharing the opportunity. A common problem in recruiting is having many people sitting on the fence.

All we need to know is the ONE thing stopping them from joining and start making money. Once we know what that is, we can conquer the objection together.

This simple question is a game changer! Are you ready to make a change in your recruiting process? Let's get those fence-sitters off the fence and onto your team.

Know the No

We can't read minds to figure out why someone doesn't sign up when we believe the opportunity is a great fit for them. We need to be prepared and understand their "NO," known as the objection. Sometimes it's simple, like not having enough time, or it could be that they don't know enough people.

Stepping out of your comfort zone helps you grow and builds confidence. Our biggest fear is rejection. I haven't met anyone who has died because someone told them "no." It's not lethal. Just learn not to take it personally and understand that "no" might mean: "Know...I need to know more" or "No...not yet."

When I coach someone on my team who's afraid of receiving a "no" and the rejection that comes with it, I ask them to think about this: When you go out to eat and the server offers dessert, have you ever said, "No thank you, I'm full"? How do you think the server feels when you say no? Do they start crying and quit because you said no? Of course not. We say no all the time. Employees are paid to ask each customer a question, and no matter the answer, they keep asking. It's a numbers game. The more you ask, the more no's you'll get, but you'll also start getting more yes's!

The "no" can change over time. I tell my team that just because it's a "no" right now doesn't mean it won't become a "yes." Think of it like

Thanksgiving Day. I always say "no" to pumpkin pie when it's first offered because I'm too stuffed after dinner. But that "no" doesn't last long. After resting and enjoying the day, I'm ready for that piece of pumpkin pie! Just because someone is "full" right now doesn't mean they'll be full all day. It's important to understand why they said "no" so you can follow up and ask again later.

Coach Rob's Notes: "Tracy nailed it! Don't be offended because someone said no. Sometimes we just need a little perspective. The fear of rejection is one of the greatest fears we all have. It ties right into the mother of all fears! The fear of judgment. Getting over yourself and these basic common fears are crucial to your success."

It took me years of practice. It didn't come naturally to me. Even after I had success, I still was very sensitive to no's because I am a recovering people pleaser! Lol!

Rise Above

My miracle story is a testament to how Network Marketing can change your life. Due to situations outside of my control, my life took a turn for the worst. With all my years of experience, one day I ended up with a j-o-b working as a cook in our ferry system. After months of treading water, there I was, packing my car with four boxes of belongings and my dog. I had lost everything: My home, stability, and most importantly, my sense of security. There aren't enough words to describe how hard this hit me. I became homeless and moved in with my mom. It was during this time that I heard about a new, soon to launch, Network Marketing company.

It was years of work, failures, successes, and challenges that led me here. I saw the vision within what this new company had, and I jumped on board and shouted YES! Two months after that company launched and my business was growing, I found the book The Game of Networking. This book was (is) a game-changer and I can honestly say that my business would not be where it is today had I not found Rob Sperry and his book.

I linked arms with Rob Sperry, attended his masterminds, leaned into his mentorship, and took advantage of his trainings and coaching. This guidance help me build a team of over 40,000 members and brought me from homeless to an annual 7-figure income.

CONCLUSION

As we conclude "Mastering Network Marketing: Proven Approaches from Greats," I hope you feel empowered and equipped with the knowledge to transform your network marketing business. The insights and strategies shared by the industry leaders featured in this book are not just theoretical concepts; they are proven methods that have helped countless individuals achieve remarkable success.

Remember, the key to mastering network marketing lies in continuous learning and adaptation. Stay curious, keep refining your skills, and always be open to new ideas. The journey to success is ongoing, and each step you take brings you closer to your goals.

Thank you for joining me on this journey. I am confident that with the right mindset, dedication, and the strategies outlined in this book, you can achieve great things in network marketing. Now, go out there and create the success you deserve!

www.ingramcontent.com/pod-product-compliance
Lightning Source LLC
Chambersburg PA
CBHW041209220326
41597CB00030BA/5162